A Pencil in God's Hand

Prayer Reflections

❧

by Zeca Rodrigues

DORRANCE
PUBLISHING CO
EST. 1920
PITTSBURGH, PENNSYLVANIA 15238

Dorrance Publishing Co
585 Alpha Drive
Suite 103
Pittsburgh, PA 15238
Visit our website at www.dorrancebookstore.com

ISBN: 978-1-6491-3794-4
eISBN: 978-1-6491-3982-5

CONTENTS

FOREWORD

This book is written because of the repeated requests of my family and friends with whom I have shared some inspirational messages after immersing myself into the gospel readings to try and get to know Jesus, my friend and my God. After much prayer as to whether or not these messages were private messages for me alone and discerning whether they should be shared, I woke up one morning with the thought, *Share them, be a pencil in God's Hand.* I realized that I had heard this phrase just a few days before while watching a documentary on Mother Theresa, where she referred to herself as "a pencil in the hand of God." I took this as confirmation that God wanted me to share these inspirational messages in book form, and He even provided the title.

1.

A CALL TO PRAYER

My prayer journey has always been filled with many ups and downs. I have experienced some half-hearted moments, some incredible moments and some very dark moments. My half-hearted moments were the times in my life where I knew God existed, my faith told me so, but I had no personal experience of Him, and He seemed way too distant for me to have a relationship with Him. My incredible moments were times when I witnessed true miracles that I had no doubt God was alive and well and living among us. From time to time, I experienced some very dark moments. The absence of God. Times when I doubted everything, times when prayers seemed to have no meaning, and times when I wanted nothing to do with praying. Looking back, it is clear that it has been after enduring the darkest moments when I have grown more profoundly in my faith and have been invited to a more personal relationship with Jesus.

I am a cradle Catholic, and I love being Catholic. I was born and grew up in a very small village called Paul do Mar, in Madeira Island, Portugal. Growing up, and for most of my life, my mother was my mentor. She was a very simple but very wise woman with a heart of gold. Always helping people but never talking about what she did. She loved God above all things, that was very evident. She made sure I attended catechism and learned all the prayers; memorized them well. I could recite them all. We often prayed the Rosary together as a family. Being Portuguese, the Rosary was particularly important to us because of the apparitions of Our Lady of Fatima in Portugal and Our Lady's specific request to pray the Rosary. I went to Mass every Sunday and on holy days of obligation. I listened to the readings at Mass, and I knew they came from the Bible, but I had never opened a Bible. I recall seeing a Bible at home respectfully placed on a small table, in a place of honor, but I don't think I had ever even touched it. The Bible was holy, it was sacred, and it wasn't for me to touch it. Who knows what would have happened if I did!

I immigrated to the United States when I was 15 years old. Truly blessed, we came to live in San Diego, California, where there was a very well-established Portuguese community. Our faith practices continued to be familiar to what I had been brought up with. Through high school and then college, I felt myself distancing a bit. I thought I didn't really have to go to Mass every Sunday. It just wasn't that important, and I wasn't very interested. However, looking back, I know that God kept tugging at my heart strings. I would attend Mass at the Newman Center at U.C. Berkeley campus, very sporadically. When I first moved into my own apartment, in Hayward, California, my next-door neighbor was a little old lady who always had Bible in hand and always wanted to talk to me about Jesus. I didn't want to be disrespectful, but I really didn't know what she was talking about. She called herself a Christian. I was Catholic and, because of my naiveté at best, I didn't think the two could mix.

After graduating college and traveling the world for a whole year on a college student budget, I returned to San Diego eager to start working. Out of respect for my mother, I returned to church but my feelings were the same; a little empty, devoid of any significance.

A few years later, my best friend Bela told me she wanted to get confirmed. I was a little puzzled since it would mean she would have to attend classes (catechism) for one or two years to be confirmed. She was already an adult, and I could not understand why she would want to do that. But, it was important to her, so I supported her and even became her sponsor/godmother. On the big day, when she was confirmed by the Bishop at St. Agnes Catholic Church, we had planned to go out after the ceremony with some friends and party. Just as we walked outside, a Portuguese lady named Dorie Valin walked up to my friend and congratulated her on this very special day and how the Holy Spirit had truly blessed her! We looked at each other and were truly puzzled. We both knew of Dorie, but didn't really know her. Also, I know Dorie was speaking English, but her language was completely foreign to me. Dorie continued talking to us about Jesus as if He was her best friend. This woman is Catholic, she's Portuguese, I knew this. What is she talking about? Needless to say, a spark was lit inside of us. We forgot about the party and were mesmerized by her stories. We soaked in her every word. We wanted to hear about this Jesus she seemed to know so much about. She invited us to her house, and she talked for hours. She showed us her Bible. Her Bible was obviously well loved and well used. It was underlined everywhere, full of tabs and bookmarks on almost every page. She had us hold it and read from it. She showed us that in the Bible, there were lots of books, each telling us the story of God. She showed us how our Catholic Mass is a true collection of prayers right out of the Bible. She even read the same readings they had read in church when Bela was confirmed! Then, she prayed. Not the memorized prayers we all knew but spontaneous prayers from the heart – she was having a conversation with God! Inviting the Holy Spirit to fill us. Acknowledging Jesus' presence in our midst. This was personal. That day completely changed my life and my relationship with God.

In the days that followed, we called some friends and told them of our encounter with Dorie. They all agreed to ask Dorie to teach us more. We formed a Bible study group, the first one I had ever attended. We were introduced to the Catholic Charismatic Renewal movement. Outsiders would often referred to this movement as the "Happy Catholics" and sometimes the "Crazy Catholics." Whatever the label, I was okay with it. "Jesus is alive and well and living among us" was my new motto. I became a certified catechist and taught religious education for many years at Saint Agnes as well as at Ascension Catholic Parish, teaching seventh graders and then confirmation and post-confirmation teens, for many years. I attended and participated in many retreats. I even chaperoned several groups of teenagers and attended St. Pope John Paul II's World Youth Days in Denver, Colorado, and in Rome, Italy. I wanted our youth to be as excited about Jesus as I was. I wanted to re-assure them they did not have to seek other Christian faiths to get to know Jesus[1]. I wanted them to realize how our memorized prayers were but a step in our relationship with Jesus. When prayed from the heart instead of the mind these were all beautiful prayers. Most were actually Bible verses (the Our Father, the Hail Mary). I wanted them to get to know and meet the person of Jesus.

One year, as a class project, I decided to go off text, off the lesson plan. I told my seventh graders we were going to learn about the Stations of the Cross – Jesus' Way of the Cross. All were familiar with what they were, and I saw some students roll their eyes. I gave them each a piece of paper with a title – The (*blank*)____ Station. I had posters of each one of the stations laid out around the room. I had each student pull a number from a basket to get their "station" assignment. Then, they were to fill out the number of their assigned blank station; look at the corresponding poster; research the Bible

---

[1] During this time there was an alarming exodus of Catholics moving to New Horizons Christian Church.

to find the corresponding passage; write down the scripture reference and text; and finally, make up their own prayer. Lastly, they were to answer one question in writing: "How did this particular station relate to your own life today? Class time was up before we had a chance to share them in class. I collected their assignment and wished them a good week. Later that night, I read them. I was completely blown away. The insight these kids had was out of this world, certainly well beyond their years! I first shared them with Dorie, who immediately asked me to put them into a booklet to be used during Lenten Service of the Stations of the Cross. Then I shared them with our Director of Religious Education at Ascension Church, Sue Paul, who was as touched as I was. The following year, Sue approached me and another catechist Linda DeGraw, proposing that we do a re-enactment of the gospel with the kids during the Good Friday Services. She already had the script – the exact gospel reading for the day – the Passion of Christ. (John 18:1-49; 19:1-42)

We invited all youth, fourth grade and up, in the parish to participate. We held try-outs, and anyone could try out for any part. Everyone who auditioned had a part. We embarked in creating very authentic wardrobe and what could not be sewn, like the Roman soldiers' garb, was rented. We had a very good reader who narrated the entire gospel reading while the play unfolded before the congregation with the assigned characters interjecting their own lines on queue. Parishioners, parents, and the kids' themselves helped with all the necessary props – the vestments, Pilate's water bowl, his towel, the whips, the crown of thorns, the sign, the hammer, the nails, the lance, the burial linens, the jar for the burial spices. My nephew, John Gibson, made a cross with a stand so that when Jesus was nailed to the cross he was elevated. The altar was our stage.

We rehearsed for several weeks. I directed the play, Linda tended to the details of the wardrobe and props, and Sue handled the administrative issues. During the first rehearsals everyone was going through the motions, acting as if they were participating in a regular play, acting out someone's life story. However, during dress rehearsal, it was amazing to see the transformation that occurred. Suddenly, there was reverence, something touched their hearts and ours. This was not just someone's life story. This was Jesus' story, and we were part of it.

I will never forget what happened during our very first re-enactment. The church was packed, mostly with extended families coming to see their kids in the play. As the narrator began, we could hear giggles and see camera flashes. The audience was bobbing up and down and heads turning as everyone was trying to find their child. Then they saw Judas betraying Jesus with a kiss. Jesus was brought before Pilate. They heard a very loud bang coming from back, the entrance door behind them, as Barabbas had been set free, and it caused the spectators to laugh a little. Pilate washed his hands, and everyone started to settle down. Then Jesus was led to the side and the scourging began. The sound of the whips resonated throughout the church and everyone stretched their necks to get a glimpse of what was happening. We heard a loud painful but contained gasp from Jesus as a soldier placed the crown of thorns on His head. And so, the congregation got a little more quiet – a little more tense. They see Jesus, bloody and frail being led by the Roman soldiers parading up and down the aisles of the church. He falls and is led back to the altar to be crucified. When He was nailed to the cross, we used a mallet and real nails for sound effects. At the same time that the mallet hit the nail and the wood of the cross, the youngster playing Jesus let out such a powerful, painful but contained cry that shook the congregation. The audience's reaction was incredible. Some let out painful sighs and gasps while others tried to contain their tears. This scene was as real as I could have ever imagined or experienced. Suddenly, when Jesus' lifeless body was brought down from the cross and put on Mary's arms (played by Linda's daughter Kirsten), she did something so powerful and unexpected of such a young teenager, that just penetrated the hearts of all those present. She cried, but a cry that could have only come from the depths of her soul. It was a wailing, a lamentation an agonizing cry that penetrated our own souls. It was controlled and angelic sounding. By this time, much of the congregation could not hold back the tears. That first year was such a moving performance by all the kids who participated that all the years that followed could not compare. Or, perhaps I was the one mostly affected by it. It was seeing this re-enactment that led me to truly think, reflect and meditate on Jesus' way of the cross more deeply.

And so in the years that followed, especially during Lent, I reflected on the Stations of the Cross. I was experiencing such a spiritual high that I never thought I would ever come off that mountain top. Then I lost myself. I went through a very difficult time spiritually, personally, financially, and emotionally. I had to change jobs. I was still praying, but I doubted God's existence. Nothing made sense. I remember thinking that I was in a deep hole – in quicksand, and the harder I tried to get out, the deeper I sank. Those dark days turned into years. I prayed and prayed. I really missed my spiritual highs when my faith felt unshakable when God was my everything. In my darkness, I just went through the motions. God was not hearing my prayers. Maybe I just complained too much. I would give permission to my negative thoughts to sink me even deeper.

In March 2011, I left a job I loved without having another job lined up. This was very uncharacteristic of me. I had worked there for 17 years, but in the last few years my boss and I had some unreconcilable views and, after much prayer and for my own sanity, I felt it was best to leave. It broke my heart because people I had loved as my own family had betrayed me. This was a very difficult time and one that ruined me financially. I should have left a year earlier, but I didn't. I was always hoping things would change, and when I realized they weren't going to I just took my losses and left. As God would have it, a few months later, I was hired by a firm that had split from my old boss. I am grateful to say I am still holding that job today.

For most of 2011, as I began to recover emotionally, the reality of my dire financial situation was very clear, and I began to doubt my decisions. I doubted God. I wondered if God existed. I had prayed and prayed, but how could He have allowed all this to happen? I tried to pray, but I didn't know how and wondered if it even mattered. Did God hear my prayers?

In August of the same year, I visited a friend who had gone through a divorce. While sharing our situations and disappointments, we both felt we were lost souls. We reminisced of our Bible study group at Dorie's and what it meant to us. We decided that we should meet on a weekly basis to try and get into scripture again. We needed help. Our meetings only lasted about a month. However, in the few times I had prepared for our meetings, I came to listen to Joel Osteen and was introduced to Joyce Meyer. They inspired me to start praying again and to journal. I journaled every day, faithfully, until 2013. Some days, I would journal for hours. In the years that followed, although I didn't journal every day, I continued some journaling.

During this time, I actually read the entire Old Testament. I was truly amazed how there was always a message for me relevant to my life that day. I was ready and eager to start the New Testament, read it from beginning to end, but I didn't. I stopped. I can't pinpoint any specific reason why I stopped, but I did. I tried but just couldn't get into it. I felt lost. My prayer life was again a huge void. At times, I felt I didn't know how to pray or what to pray for. I know I prayed. I went to Mass. I followed the readings (scripture), but there was a disconnect between my heart and my soul. I re-read past journal entries, I listened to podcasts, I tried to read scripture, but nothing "clicked." As I look back now, I recall talking to a friend about my lack of interest in journaling after I had been so good for so many years and how inspirational it had been, and she said, "Maybe you need to write a book. Maybe you already have everything you need in those past entries." (I just remembered this memory now as I'm writing this down.)

Finally, one day, just before Lent in 2018, I decided to talk to our pastor, Father Don Coleman. I was having a soul crisis, and maybe he could offer me some insight just as we were getting ready for Lent. Our meeting was brief, but he suggested I listen to a podcast by Matthew Kelly of Dynamic Catholic called Best Lent Ever. I wasn't exactly thrilled, but I thought I would give it a try since he had recommended. The messages were short and simple and very profound. I listened to them every day. I even picked up the Bible, but a few verses into whatever chapter I happened to read, I was distracted and respectfully put it away. But I kept trying even as my head kept dissuading me. I was alerted to listen to Best Advent Ever 2018 and Best Lent Ever 2019. I followed them and was enjoying them. However, my own prayer time struggles continued. I wanted to read the Bible but just could not get into it!

$\mathscr{2.}$

Rediscover Jesus – The Book

From time to time, Dynamic Catholic would mail out to me books on various topics. Most of the time I would browse through them and then put them away somewhere. Sometime in 2019, I received a book called Rediscover Jesus by Matthew Kelly. This book had such an impact on my life that I felt compelled to write the author to let him know (something I don't usually do). This book is the reason I am reading the Bible again and what taught me to be totally available to God in prayer, which then allowed God to gift me with "these" inspirational moments. This is part of the email I sent to Matthew Kelly at Dynamic Catholic on January 23, 2020:

> *I just wanted to thank you for the Rediscover Jesus book! It has truly "transformed" my life. For almost two years I struggled with my prayer life. Prayer, in any form, just seemed meaningless. I couldn't get into reading the Bible and even listening to the readings at mass just didn't seem to make much sense. Then, sometime ago Dynamic Catholic sent me your Rediscover Jesus book. I placed it on my night stand and left it there for quite some time.*

The day after Thanksgiving (2019) I had to fly to Oakland for a family matter. I don't know why I grabbed the book but I did and put it in my purse. While on the plane, I reached into my purse to grab my phone so I could play my usual video game. I couldn't find my phone but realized I had the book in hand. I started flipping through it then I thought I needed to read it. I couldn't put it down and I never did, until I landed in Oakland. On the way back from Oakland I picked up the book and finished it. I found myself praying the Transformation prayer over and over. Something within me was changing. I couldn't quite understand what. When I read the chapter on "Delve into the Gospels" I felt an immediate call to prayer. I truly felt God was inviting me to devote time to prayer. I had read in the book that if we want to get closer to God then we need to know the God-Jesus and the best way to know Jesus is to read the gospels but, not to just read them, but to first read it then go back and immerse ourselves in it. That night I actually went into prayer reflecting on the many messages in your book. Right there and then I planned my prayer commitment for Advent, which included your Best Advent Ever series. I felt a deep desire to do exactly what you had suggested – read the gospels; get to know Jesus through the gospels…

3.

READING THE GOSPELS

And so, it began. On December 2, 2019, as I was driving to work, I got to the traffic light at the intersection of Byron and Rosecrans, and I felt I was "being reminded" to go to St. Agnes Church and read the Bible like it had been suggested by Matthew Kelly. The church was just a few blocks away. I turned the corner and did as I was being "asked."

While in prayer, I asked God to bring someone or something to life so that I could expand my idea of the events at the time and learn about Jesus and everyone in His life.

I read the entire Chapter 1 of Matthew's gospel because it is the first gospel. It starts off with the genealogy of Jesus – the father of this one, the father of this one, the father... and already I was getting bored. Then, almost instantly, I thought about how excited I get when working on my own genealogy and how important it is to make these connections. Suddenly, I didn't mind reading about it and actually became keenly interested and was able to finish the entire chapter. Back at Saint Agnes, after reading Matthew 1, I started thinking of all the events in that chapter.

I started summarizing them in my head and later I wrote them down:

Genealogy of Jesus (Matthew 1:1 – 1:17)
  14 generations from Abraham to David
  14 generations from David to Exile to Babylon
  14 generations from Exile to Babylon to the Birth of Jesus

Birth of Jesus (Matthew 1:18-25)
  Mary was found with child
  Joseph wanted to send her away and break their engagement
  Joseph has a dream. The angel said "the child in her womb is of the Holy Spirit"
  She will have a son and you shall call him Jesus he shall save his people from their sins
  All came to pass to fulfill what the prophet had said "...the virgin shall be with child and shall bear a son, and they shall call his name Emmanuel...God with us."

I returned to the church the next day. Read the entire chapter again and suddenly, while still in prayer, my thoughts were not my own. In my head were thoughts as if I was Joseph. I was thinking in the first person, but I was Joseph. I felt a little strange and, after a while, decided to leave church, thinking I was being distracted. I got in my car, and my thoughts were still Joseph. When I centered myself for my evening prayer, Joseph was still in my head. When I woke up the next morning, Joseph was still there. Anytime I was alone, a continuation of Joseph's thoughts filled my head. The next day, I went back to church, and I started reading Matthew 2 as the logical progression, yet I felt compelled to re-read Matthew 1. This went on for a few days. I was stuck in Matthew 1, and Joseph was stuck in my head. I began to wonder what I was missing here – what was

God trying to tell me that I just didn't get? I decided I should write Joseph's thoughts down, whatever I could remember. When I started typing, it was as if every detail was being dictated to me. When I finished writing Joseph, all his thoughts went away.

When I read the message I had typed up, I was pleasantly surprised. The insight was not my own. I was a little scared because perhaps my head was playing tricks on me. Was Satan messing up with my mind? Was this really from God? I prayed about it and decided to share it with my sister. She's always my go-to. She was amazed. As she put it – she has read or heard that story so many times, but this message really spoke to her. It made her understand what was happening. She wanted me to share more messages as I got them. In fact, she said I should write a book because she knew other people would love to hear these messages because it would lead them to want to read scripture and understand. Then she told a mutual friend about it, and she wanted to hear them. These became our prayer time. Then my sister had me share them with her kids and encouraged me to share with others. Everyone's reaction was the same. They started asking me if they could share it with their friends. Then I felt comfortable enough to share with some of my own friends. Some wanted the messages printed out, so they could read these inspirational moments (as I called them) on their own. I hesitated but after much prayer I feel God wants these to be shared. If these messages can bring just one person to read scripture, to know Jesus, then I believe God's desire is being fulfilled.

As I mentioned before, this type of prayer was not completely foreign to me because, in 2012 and 2013, I had been led to pray the (Catholic) Stations of the Cross by immersing myself in each scene. Those were very powerful prayerful moments, and so I gladly welcomed these new inspirational moments.

I prayed the entire month of December and into mid-January, one chapter per day from Matthew and Luke's gospels. I read and re-read the same chapter over and over and wrote down each inspired moment. Suffice it to say, I only read Matthew 1 and 2 and Luke 1 and 2 the entire time. During this time, I received some very profound prayerful inspirational moments, which I am sharing here. The scriptural references here are from the Catholic Public Domain Version Bible.

4.

IMMERSING MYSELF
"DELVING" INTO THE GOSPELS

These inspirational moments are prayer moments. In my journal, I not only write down the Biblical reference corresponding to the event, but I write the actual scriptural text referenced. I urge the reader, as you prepare yourself to read these inspirational moments, to first read the referenced scripture passage or the entire chapter as an opening prayer. Who knows, you may be lead on your own journey of inspired moments as well. Also, at the end of each of these Moments, I pose three questions to personalize the message: What is this telling me? How does it apply to my life? What have I learned about Jesus? I ask these questions only after I have finished writing down the entire message.

I do not decide what character comes through. I read the entire chapter then my thoughts are consumed by the one character. Sometimes it takes several days sometimes right away. The thoughts of the character remain in my head until I write them down. That, too, can be one day or several days. Only after I write it down am I able to move on. In the case of Matthew 1, which starts with the genealogy of Jesus then jumps right into Mary being with child and Joseph's struggles, in the normal progression of things, I would go on to Matthew 2. However, Matthew 2 goes right into the Magi, Herod, the flight to Egypt. It was as if I was reading the end of story and completely missed the beginning and the middle. That soft inner whisper in my heart led me to jump to Luke 1 before reading Matthew 2, and just like that, the gap was filled. Like before, I read and re-read the entire chapter of Luke 1. Similar to my experience with Joseph, Mary was in my head. My thoughts were her thoughts. Mary was coming through loud and clear. I wrote them down and then they went away. Then, Zechariah came through, Elizabeth came then Joseph again talking about taking Mary to Bethlehem. These were some very powerful message for me, and I was totally fascinated by them especially as I re-read them. I was so excited about reading the Bible. Then, I began to worry. Was this me on an ego trip, or were these truly divine inspirations? I let these doubts sink in.

I continued reading the Bible, but no one was coming through. I feared they had stopped. I missed them. It had been well over a week since any character had come through. Nonetheless, I continued reading the Bible, but I was stuck on Luke 1.

I stopped by the church one morning, and just then, Father Don saw me and asked how I was doing. I briefly shared with him about these personal inspirational messages and how I was just on top of the world but, I told him, I was doubting if they were truly from God or my head. He simply said, "Wasn't this what you had been praying for? A personal relationship with Jesus? Be careful what you pray for. Sometimes God just amazes us." Amazed I was. Father left. I knelt down to pray. I re-read Luke 1 then Matthew 2. Suddenly, something very strange happened. While in meditation, I took on the persona of the star. I found it quite an interesting perspective and didn't really know where it would lead me. I started thinking that perhaps the Magi would come through, but no! I was the star. Not just any star, but the star that guided the Magi to Jesus. This was so out of left field that I thought – *Only God!* I believe this was God's way of showing me that these inspirations are His and not mine. While still reading Matthew 2, I was also led to read Luke 2. Then, the shepherds came, Simeon, the Magi, Joseph again (the flight to Egypt), Herod, and Mary. I wasn't really being led to read Matthew 3 or Luke 3. I was sure I was to continue reading Matthew 2 and Luke 2. During this time, as most of the characters in those chapters had made their presence, I started thinking about the role of the angels and of dreams in them. I got excited and couldn't wait for the next message which would surely be about one of these. Or, perhaps about the "things Mary pondered in her heart." These were the only ones missing, I thought. Over a week went by and nothing. In mid-January, I was again nudged, while running some errands in the middle of the afternoon, to stop by the church and spend a little quiet time with God. I thanked God for these revelations and decided to look up Matthew 3, Luke 3, and Mark 1 which all started with John the Baptist. I read all three chapters, but I didn't feel led to meditate on those just yet. So, I jumped on to John 1. John's gospel starts with "In the beginning was the Word..." Immediately, I began to reflect again on the genealogy of Jesus and I recalled vividly the passages in Matthew 1 as well as what I had just read in Luke 3. In John 1, Jesus' genealogy is tied to God Himself. He is the Word. Suddenly, I realized that in Matthew 1, the genealogy of Jesus is traced back to Abraham, through Solomon the son of David (Matthew 1:1-17). In Luke 3, His genealogy is traced all the way back to Adam, the son of God, through Nathan the son of David (Luke 3:23-38). And, in the gospel of John, Jesus is the Word – God Himself (John 1:1-5). I had never made this connection nor had I ever heard it before, but I was utterly amazed to have received this revelation.

The following day, I had to travel to Tijuana, Mexico (about a 45-minute drive each way). I stopped by St. Agnes to say a little prayer before I went. There He was – the exposition of the Blessed

Sacrament. This would be equivalent to being in the Holy of Holies, right before the Arc of the Covenant. I did some personal prayer and started to think about Mary, the angels, and dreams as the things I would, most certainly, be called to reflect upon. Nothing came to mind. Then, that very familiar faint voice came through. I felt as though God was thanking me for being bold to share the messages. I was humbled and overjoyed all at once. God was thanking me! I was very happy I had followed through on God's request to share the messages and felt confident these were His messages.

I continued in prayer and thought I would be led to meditate on Mary and the things she pondered in her heart. And, just as I centered myself and readied for whatever – the thoughts cleared, and I was the donkey! I was a little frustrated because I thought these were distractions invading my prayer time, and I kept trying to get them out of my mind. But I was the donkey, and there were no other thoughts coming through. I thought my prayer time was over with all these "distractions," because I couldn't think of anything else but the donkey, and so I got up and got in my car. The thoughts of the donkey came along! In the long ride to Tijuana, I opened up to the thoughts about the donkey to see where it led me or maybe they would go away. They didn't. The donkey was in my head for days. Scenes picked up where they had left off. When I went to prayer or anytime when I was alone, the friendly donkey was in my head. I finally wrote these thoughts down. To say that I was amazed is to put it lightly. What an interesting perspective! We are all God's creatures, and we all have a purpose in life. Like with the star, I knew this could have only come from God.

5.

INSPIRATIONAL MOMENTS – THE MESSAGES

I am sharing here the messages I had written down in my journal. I hope these are a blessing to you as they have been to me. The messages listed here are in the order received and not in chronological order.

JOSEPH – MARY IS WITH CHILD

Now the procreation of the Christ occurred in this way. After his mother Mary had been betrothed to Joseph, before they lived together, she was found to have conceived in her womb by the Holy Spirit. Then Joseph, her husband, since he was just and was not willing to hand her over, preferred to send her away secretly. But while thinking over these things, behold, an Angel of the Lord appeared to him in his sleep, saying: "Joseph, son of David, do not be afraid to accept Mary as your wife. For what has been formed in her is of the Holy Spirit. And she shall give birth to a son. And you shall call his name JESUS. For he shall accomplish the salvation of his people from their sins." Now all this occurred in order to fulfill what was spoken by the Lord through the prophet, saying: "Behold, a virgin shall conceive in her womb, and she shall give birth to a son. And they shall call his name Emmanuel, which means: God is with us." Then Joseph, arising from sleep, did just as the Angel of the Lord had instructed him, and he accepted her as his wife. And he knew her not, yet she bore her son, the firstborn. And he called his name JESUS. (Matthew 1:18-25)

I am Joseph. I am at work doing my carpentry as I have done for many years. I love my work and love creating something out of a piece of wood. These days, however, my workday feels so much longer than before. My head is filled with thoughts of Mary, my fiancée. I feel like a mere thought of her brings a smile to my face, and it warms my heart. I can't wait to go see Mary. I can't believe Mary accepted to be my wife. I can't believe Mary said yes. I am truly the happiest man on this Earth. My days are so filled with excitement and joy, and all I can think about is spending the rest of my days with Mary, caring for her, being with her, loving her. Mary was everything I had hoped for. She had tremendous faith, and she loved God above all things. She was not only beautiful on the outside, but her inner beauty surpassed it by far. I expected her to be a fervent woman of God because I know her parents consecrated her to the Lord when she was very young, and she grew up learning scripture even better than most men. God was her compass. He was the center of her life in everything. I am indeed truly blessed!

And so, as I always did at the end of my day, I stopped by her house to see her. When I entered the house, I was not greeted with the same enthusiasm I had been received before. I sensed something was wrong; Mary was sitting, and she wouldn't look at me. My heart was breaking in pieces. I wondered if she had changed her mind. I wanted to ask what was wrong, but the words would not come out or maybe I was afraid to find out. I started walking towards Mary, but I didn't want to scare her more than she already looked. This was all very troubling. What could possibly be wrong? What did I do? How do I fix it?

Suddenly, Ana (Mary's mother) grabbed my arm and led me to the side, across from Mary. She said something to me, but nothing registered. I looked at her face, and there was so much sadness. She waited for my response, but I wasn't quite sure what I had heard. Then she repeated and I heard, "She's with child!" I raised my voice and looking at Ana and then to Mary I said: "What do you mean she's with child? I haven't touched her. How could she be with child?!" My mind was racing a mile a minute. How could I wrap all this in my head? What am I going to do? I need to terminate our engagement. I told her mother perhaps we should send her far away. Ana was saddened and asked that I should listen to Mary and have her explain, but I didn't want to hear it. I started thinking what people would do to Mary when they found out. She could be stoned to death! But, I didn't want to hear anything. Ana said something about Mary being visited by an angel, and that's how she got pregnant, by the Holy Spirit. I really wasn't up to hearing a story like that! It just seemed a little farfetched.

I left Mary's house. I started on my way home. The pain in my heart was too much to bear. What had I done to deserve this? If she didn't want to be with me, why did she accept to be my wife. She seemed so happy when I asked. What has gone wrong? How could Mary have done this to me? This story about the angel and the Holy Spirit – who would believe it? That's crazy! I wanted to cry, and started wondering if perhaps I had heard everything wrong, but everything was running through my head as if I could see it happening all over again. I was sure I had heard well.

I must have been walking through the streets aimlessly, and as I lifted my head to get my bearings to see where I was, I realized that I was right in front of the temple, which is in the opposite direction of my house. I felt I needed to pray. I just needed to talk to

God and figure this out. I thought I should go and talk to my Rabi; surely he would counsel me on what I needed to do. I was convinced Mary loved God above all things. It was one of the qualities that had attracted me to her. I know (as a people) we the Israelites are waiting for the Messiah to come and save us, but God is choosing to be born like a human? Shouldn't He just appear in His glory and lead us all to paradise? What do I do? If I tell the Rabi, will he be compelled to share it with the other members of the temple? How will they deal with Mary? What will they do to her? How would all of this affect Mary? She would be disgraced. Although I was very hurt and heartbroken, I loved Mary, and I didn't want anything bad to happen to her. I wasn't sure I wanted to go see the Rabi after all, and just as I was about to turn around and go home, the Rabi sees me and calls me over. He could sense there was something troubling me. I asked him about the Messiah; what did he know about His coming. The Rabi seemed puzzled with my line of questioning, but he simply reminded me that according to the prophesies, the Messiah would be born of a virgin. As he said that, I realized that I had read this prophesy many times before in the book of the prophet Isaiah, which said, "the Lord himself will give you a sign: The virgin will be with child and will give birth to a son, and you will call him Emmanuel." I knew this to be true but surely this is not what was happening here. My heart found no consolation, and surprisingly, without asking another question, the Rabi told me that I should go home, take my concerns to the Lord, and come back the next day to see him if I needed to.

I was a little put off by his dismissal because this was an emergency; I needed to send Mary away. But I went home. I prayed that God enlighten me; what should I do? Where should I send Mary? What explanation was I going to give the people? What was going to happen to Mary? I thought and I thought and I thought that I fell asleep. Then, I had a dream. In it, an angel appeared and said he was a messenger from God. God wanted me to know that the child Mary was carrying was by the Holy Spirit; that I was not to be afraid to take Mary as my wife; that she would give birth to a son; that I was to call the child Jesus because he was coming to save his people from their sins. I woke up, and I had no doubts.

I was so excited that I ran to the Rabi to tell him, and I told him the whole story. The Rabi smiled and immediately started praying that the fulfillment of the prophesy was at hand. He had no doubts. Then I ran to Mary's and told her about my dream and immediately picked up on our plans to marry as soon as possible.

Mary immediately started praising God, for she knew that because she was telling the truth, God would take care of enlightening me. She was so sure that she never really worried for herself, but she was concerned for me. I was so overwhelmed with happiness that I would be sharing my life with Mary. When I realized the incredible events unfolding before our eyes, I was overcome with humility. I realized I was chosen to take care of the Son of God! What had I done to deserve such an honor? My heart swelled with joy, and I couldn't believe all that was happening. Then, I sat down and listened to all that had happened to Mary; her encounter with the angel and all he had told her; how she accepted this incredible responsibility simply because God asked her to without caring about what would happen to her; revealing her undeniable faith, her love for God and for all humanity. Mary certainly could never imagine where life would lead us but one thing she was sure – God is in control. He was guiding us and we would follow his guidance unconditionally.

What is this telling me?
How does it apply to my life?
What have I learned about Jesus here?

MARY – THE ANNUNCIATION

Then, in the sixth month, the Angel Gabriel was sent by God, to a city of Galilee named Nazareth, to a virgin betrothed to a man whose name was Joseph, of the house of David; and the name of the virgin was Mary. And upon entering, the Angel said to her: "Hail, full of grace, The Lord is with you. Blessed are you among women." And when she had heard this, she was disturbed by his words, and she considered what kind of greeting this might be. And the Angel said to her: "Do not be afraid, Mary, for you have found grace with God. Behold, you shall conceive in your womb, and you shall bear a son, and you shall call his name: JESUS. He will be great, and he will be called the Son of the Most High, and the Lord God will give him the throne of David his father. And he will reign in the house of Jacob for eternity. And his kingdom shall have no end." Then Mary said to the Angel, "How shall this be done, since I do not know man? And in response, the Angel said to her: "The Holy Spirit will pass over you, and the power of the Most High will overshadow you. And because of this also, the Holy One who will be born of you shall be called the Son of God. And behold, your cousin Elizabeth has herself also conceived a son, in her old age. And this is the sixth month for her who is called barren. For no word will be impossible with God." Then, Mary said: Behold, I am the handmaid of the Lord. Let it be done to me according to your word." And the Angel departed from her. (Luke 1:26-38)

I woke up this morning, praising God for all the wonderful things about to unfold today.

Like all my days, I spent time in prayer as soon as I woke up. Today my thoughts centered on the greatness of the Lord. I couldn't put into words exactly what I was feeling, but I sensed something incredible was about to happened. I felt the power of God surrounding me, surrounding this place. I couldn't wait to see what God had planned for me today. Mother had gone to the market early in the morning. I started to do my chores and was sweeping the floor, singing songs of praise from my lips. Suddenly, there was a tremendous light in the room. I was startled. I looked at the door and the window and couldn't figure out where this beautiful light was coming from. Almost instantly, the light took the shape of a majestic being, a beautiful angel. His face was the most beautiful face I had ever seen. His eyes pierced my heart, and although his lips were not moving, I could hear him say, "Hail, full of grace, the Lord is with you, blessed are you among women!" I was confused and a little afraid. Why would this angelic being address me in such a way? What kind of greeting was this? He read my thoughts and immediately told me not to be afraid. He said that I had found favor with God, that I have been chosen. He said I would conceive and bear a son, and I was to call him Jesus. He will be great, a savior to our people Israel. He will be the Son of God. He continued on that God will give him the throne of David and that He will reign in the house of Jacob forever, and His kingdom will have no end. This was an incredible message. I, Mary of Nazareth, have been chosen by God to deliver to the world, God the Savior of our people, the promised Messiah. But, how could I have a baby if I have never been with a man? Immediately, the angel said, "the Holy Spirit will pass over you and the power of the Most High will overshadow you, and the one who will be born of you shall be the Son of God." I was marveling in this message, trying to understand how this could be happening to me, a poor lowly girl. I was humbled by the visit of the angel and his message. Then, as if to give me something to hang on to, the angel added that my cousin Elizabeth, who was already of an advanced age, well beyond child bearing age and who everyone knew had never conceived a child and would never conceive a child, was already in her sixth month. What incredible news this was. My poor cousin who had lived a life of shame and disgrace had been blessed by God and was indeed going to have a child.

The angel said, "Nothing is impossible with God!" And I was sure this to be true. Immediately, using my own words I told him, my response to God was, "I am the handmaid of the Lord, be it done to me according to Your word!" I accept! I am ready to be used according to God's plan. Suddenly, as if the breath of God sucked in the light surrounding me, the angel departed.

I don't really know how long this visit from the angel lasted. I started to think about what had just happened. There was such immense peace and joy and love in my heart. All I wanted to do was praise God! My soul was filled with the presence of God. I recited all the prophesies relating to the coming of the Messiah. "Behold, a virgin shall conceive in her womb and she shall give birth to a son." I am a virgin, and the angel said I would be giving birth to a son. I am a virgin, engaged to Joseph, and I have not known man. How was I going to explain this to Joseph? What would I tell my mother? I trust that all that has just unfolded is from God, and so I trust God implicitly, and He will make things right. I prayed and praised and asked for God's guidance with every word I was to tell my mother. I trust the Lord that she will believe.

Mother returned from the market, and when she looked at me, she knew something had happened. She asked if I had been sleeping or if I had, had a vision because my face was so radiant, and my entire being was glowing. I immediately told my mother what had happened and what the angel had said. My mother is a very pious and righteous woman. She did not say a word but embraced me and assured me that everything was going to be fine. She proclaimed, "If God appoints, He anoints!" She was as concerned for Joseph as was I. What would we tell him? How would we tell him? What would he do? A million and one questions running through our heads. We knelt and prayed. We felt God wanted us to wait until he came home a little later. We would tell him the truth, exactly how it happened. As I sat in prayer and waiting for Joseph to come home, I started thinking about how this would affect Joseph. Would he reject me or would he see that he, too, was chosen by God to care for the Son of God! Would he see this as a great gift or a curse? I prayed and prayed, and I trusted God would take care of everything. What if Joseph decided to break our engagement? What would the people do to me? What would happen to me. Then, I remembered what the angel had said: "nothing is impossible with God!" I just need to trust that God is in control. I don't know how all of this will unfold, but I do know that the hand of God is orchestrating these events, and they will be fulfilled according to His will. I continued in prayer. I was absolutely astonished that I had been chosen to be the mother of our Savior. God was entrusting me with His Son. The angel's salutation sunk in "hail, full of grace, the Lord is with you, blessed are you among women!" I am full of grace carrying the Son of God in my womb. I am truly blessed among all women. I was enormously humbled by this greeting.

Suddenly, I heard Joseph's voice, so cheerful and excited. He was calling out my name as he usually did. He would take me in his arms and just spin me around full of joy. Today, however, I didn't greet him at the door, I didn't run to him as I usually did. I didn't move from the corner of the room. I couldn't bear to look at Joseph. He sensed something was wrong. His face was filled with confusion, and I could feel his heart sink. He knew something was wrong or something had happened. As Joseph started to approach me, asking what was wrong, Mother grabbed him by the arm and took him to the other side of the room. They spoke, but I'm not sure Joseph was hearing what Mother was saying. Suddenly, he raised his voice: "With child, what do you mean she's with child? I haven't touched her." I knew he was looking at me, but I didn't dare lift my head to see his face. He kept talking to Mother, and I knew he was wondering what he was going to do with me. I heard something about sending me away. He kept asking what he was going to do; how he was going to explain all of this, because people would find out. I could see that as much as he was hurting and feeling betrayed, he still loved me and didn't want anything bad to happen to me. He was very upset, he was nervous, and he was anxious. Mother told him he would understand if he let me explain. She said he needed to listen to me, so that I could tell him all that had happened. But he didn't want to hear anything I had to say. Mother continued on and said that an angel of the Lord had appeared to me and that the prophesy of the long-awaited Messiah was being revealed and fulfilled. Joseph had had enough. He stormed out of the house. I wasn't sure I would see him ever again. Mother and I went back to our prayer, glorifying God and trusting that he would make things right. It hurt my heart that Joseph had left. I truly loved him, and he was a great man, and he would be a great husband. However, God's will was first, and if Joseph was not in God's plans for me, He would provide someone to care for His Son. I needed to trust and believe!

I shared with Mother about the angel's message that cousin Elizabeth was already in her sixth month. This news seemed to confirm for Mother that all was happening according to plan, in fulfillment of scriptures of old.

> *What is this telling me?*
> *How does it apply to my life?*
> *What have I learned about Jesus here?*

ZECHARIAH – FATHER OF JOHN THE BAPTIST

There was, in the days of Herod, king of Judea, a certain priest named Zechariah, of the section of Abijah, and his wife was of the daughters of Aaron, and her name was Elizabeth. Now they were both just before God, progressing in all of the commandments and the justifications of the Lord without blame. And they had no child, because Elizabeth was barren, and they both had become advanced in years. Then it happened that, when he was exercising the priesthood before God, in the order of his section, according to the custom of the priesthood, the lot fell so that he would offer incense, entering into the temple of the Lord. And the entire multitude of the people was praying outside, at the hour of incense. Then there appeared to him an Angel of the Lord, standing at the right of the altar of incense. And upon seeing him Zechariah was disturbed, and fear fell over him. But the Angel said to him: "Do not be afraid, Zechariah, for your prayer has been heard, and your wife Elizabeth shall bear a son to you. And you shall call his name John. And there will be joy and exultation for you, and many will rejoice in his nativity. For he will be great in the sight of the Lord, and he will not drink wine or strong drink, and he will be filled with the Holy Spirit, even from his mother's womb. And he will go before him with the spirit and power of Elijah, so that he may turn the hearts of the fathers to the sons, and the incredulous to the prudence of the just, so as to prepare for the Lord a completed people." And Zechariah said to the Angel: How may I know this? For I am elderly, and my wife is advanced in years. And in response, the Angel said to him: "I am Gabriel, who stands before God, and I have been sent to speak to you, and to proclaim these things to you. And behold, you will be silent and unable to speak, until the day on which these things shall be, because you have not believed my words, which will be fulfilled in their time." And the people were waiting for Zechariah. And they wondered why he was being delayed in the temple. Then, when he came out, he was unable to speak to them. And they realized that he had seen a vision in the temple. And he was making signs to them, but he remained mute. And it happened that, after the days of his office were completed, he went away to his house...

Then they made signs to his father, as to what he wanted him to be called. And requesting a writing tablet, he wrote, saying: His name is John. And they all wondered. Then at once his mouth was opened, and his tongue loosened, and he spoke, blessing God. And fear fell upon all of their neighbors. And all these words were made known throughout all the hill country of Judea. And all those who heard it stored it up in their hearts, saying: What do you think this boy will be? And indeed, the hand of the Lord was with him. And his father Zechariah was filled with the Holy Spirit. And he prophesied, saying:

"Blessed is the Lord God of Israel. For he has visited and has wrought the redemption of his people. And he has raised up a horn of salvation for us, in the house of David his servant, just as he spoke by the mouth of his holy prophets, who are from ages past: salvation from our enemies, and from the hand of all those who hate us, to accomplish mercy with our fathers, and to call to mind his holy testament, the oath, which he swore to Abraham, our father, that he would grant to us, so that having been freed from the hand of our enemies, we may serve him without fear, in holiness and in justice before him, throughout all our days. And you, child, shall be called the prophet of the Most High. For you will go before the face of the Lord: to prepare his ways, to give knowledge of salvation to his people for the remission of their sins, through the heart of the mercy of our

God, by which, descending from on high, he has visited us, to illuminate those who sit in darkness and in the shadow of death, and to direct our feet in the way of peace."

And the child grew, and he was strengthened in spirit. And he was in the wilderness, until the day of his manifestation to Israel. (Luke 1:5-23; 62-80)

I am Zechariah. I am an old man. My wife Elizabeth and I have been married many years. We have always been very happy together, but in our hearts, there is an immense emptiness, for we have never had children. Elizabeth is barren, and she feels such shame and guilt that she has never been able to have children. We have prayed for so many years. We hoped, but it was not to be. We wondered what sin we might have committed that God was punishing us to live our lives without a child. But, now, in our very old age, we have made peace with each other and with God.

Both Elizabeth and I are very devout Jews. God and His will for us is always first. Oh, but how I wish I could console my Elizabeth. How I wish I could take away her pain. Today, I must go to the temple. My name came up, when the lots were drawn, and I must go exercise my priestly tasks in the temple and burn the incense to send our prayers to the Lord. There is a great multitude of people outside the temple walls, waiting that I lead them in prayer. I just finished incinerating the incense to the right of the altar and was about to walk away. Suddenly, standing right there, was a bright angelic being. I shouldn't be afraid, but I was. This being emanated so much peace, it is indescribable. The angel told me not to be afraid, and at that very moment, I was in awe at the site before me. He said his name was Gabriel and that he stands before the Almighty God. He had a message for me directly from God. He said that my prayers had been heard and that my wife Elizabeth would bare a son, and we were to call him John. John? We don't have any Johns in our family lineage. A son, we are so old, and Elizabeth is well beyond her childbearing years. How can this be? I hesitated. I doubted what I was hearing, and so I asked the angel Gabriel, how would I know this would really happen? I told him, as if he didn't know – we're very old. The angel said the sign would be that from this moment forward, I would not be able to utter a word. I would be silent until the day when I would see all these things come to pass. I realized I had doubted God's message. I, who believe that nothing is impossible with God, had just put limitations to His power. Then I started reliving that very moment, the incredible visit and what Gabriel said about my son. *"He shall be great in the sight of the Lord ...and he shall be filled with the Holy Spirit... He will help many of the children of Israel turn back to God and he will prepare our people for the Lord..."* (Luke 1:15-17)

My son, blessed by God to be a man of God. I searched scripture to find the many prophesies to be fulfilled. A voice heard in the desert, prepare the way of the Lord – Is my son that voice? Is he coming to prepare God's people for his coming? The long awaited Messiah? I kept searching. I was filled with an incredible sense of peace. I couldn't wait to see Elizabeth. I couldn't wait to giver her the news. We would be having a son! She was barren no more. Disgrace had no hold on our lives or our home. How would I be able to tell her all of these things? I can't speak!

I don't know how long I was in the temple but as I walked outside I could see people were wondering what had happen – why had I taken so long? As they looked at my face they could see or rather they were sure I had a vision. They wanted to know what happened so I did my best to use my hands and signs confirming that indeed I had had a vision but the details I was saving them until I see Elizabeth.

> *What is this telling me?*
> *How does it apply to my life?*
> *What have I learned about Jesus here?*

ELIZABETH – MOTHER OF JOHN THE BAPTIST

Then, after those days, his wife Elizabeth conceived, and she hid herself for five months, saying: "For the Lord did this for me, at the time when he decided to take away my reproach among men..." And in those days, Mary, rising up, traveled quickly into the hill country to a city of Judah. And she entered into the house of Zechariah, and she greeted Elizabeth. And it appeared that, as Elizabeth heard the greeting of Mary, the infant leaped in her womb, and Elizabeth was filled with the Holy Spirit. And she cried out with a loud voice and said: "Blessed are you among women, and blessed is the fruit of your womb. And how does this concern me, so that the mother of my Lord would come to me? For behold, as the voice of your greeting came to my ears, the infant in my womb leaped for joy. And blessed are you who believed, for the things that were spoken to you by the Lord shall be accomplished." And Mary said: "My soul magnifies the Lord and my spirit rejoices in God my Savior. For he looked with favor on the lowliness of his handmaid and behold henceforth all generations shall call me blessed. For he who is great has done great things for me and holy is his Name. And his mercy is from generation to generation on those who fear him. He has accomplished powerful deeds with his arm. He has scattered the arrogant in the intentions of their heart. He has deposed the powerful from their seat, and he has exalted the humble. He has filled the hungry with good things, and the rich he has sent away empty. He has taken up his servant Israel, mindful of his mercy, just as he spoke to our fathers: to Abraham and to his offspring forever." Then Mary stayed with her for about three months and then she returned to her home. Now the time for Elizabeth to give birth arrived, and she brought forth a son. And her neighbors and relatives heard that the Lord had magnified his mercy with her, and so they congratulated her. And it happened that, on the eighth day, they arrived to circumcise the boy, and they called him by his father's name, Zechariah. And in response, his mother said, "Not so, he shall be called John." And they said to her, "But there is no one among your relatives who is called by that name." Then they made signs to his father, as to what he wanted him to be called. And requesting a writing tablet, he wrote, saying: His name is John. And they all wondered. Then at once his mouth was opened, and his tongue loosened, and he spoke, blessing God. And fear fell upon all of their neighbors. And all these words were made known throughout all the hill country of Judea. And all those who heard it stored it up in their hearts, saying: What do you think this boy will be? And indeed, the hand of the Lord was with him. And his father Zechariah was filled with the Holy Spirit. (Luke 1:24-25; 39-67)

I am Elizabeth. I was in the midst of the crowd in the temple grounds when my husband Zechariah came out to lead the people in prayer. His face was glowing. Something had happened to him. He was awe struck. His assistant led the prayer, which was something highly unusual; out of the ordinary. He motioned to the crowd that he could not speak. After the prayer service, he returned to the temple to tend to his priestly duties, and I returned home. I kept wondering what could have happened to Zechariah? My mind was racing with a million and one thoughts. I couldn't wait to have Zechariah home, so he could tell me all about it; assuming he could. People around town kept talking about it. They would ask our servants if they knew anything.

Then, Zechariah finally came home. A multitude of people followed him. He kept gesturing he couldn't speak, but this only intrigued them even more. When he reached the gate, we had to shut the doors immediately behind him to stop the people from coming in. Zechariah grabbed my arm. He took me inside and making sure there was no one around he wrote down that he had been visited by an angel of God who told him that I – motioning to my belly and gesturing a pregnant stomach and then cradling his arms as if holding a baby – was going to have a baby. I couldn't believe what I was seeing! I was going to have a baby! I didn't doubt it a bit because God can do all things, but this news was absolutely incredible. This news is the best news possible. Yeah, I'm old, but God makes all things new! I no longer had to live my life in shame. I hugged my husband. I danced for joy. I praised and thanked God. I was so incredibly happy, I forgot to ask Zechariah why he couldn't speak. As best as I could gather, he signed then wrote down that the angel told him he would be silent until the baby was born. We prayed our prayers of thanksgiving and proclaimed God's goodness and power. I was already envisioning giving birth to my child – a baby boy! Zechariah and I spent our days reflecting on the scriptures and all that had been foretold. And so, it came to pass that I became pregnant. I took very good care of myself. I seldom went out, and my husband Zechariah and my servants tended to my every need. I waited with great anticipation for the day when my son would be born.

When I was already in my sixth month, I had a very special visitor. Mary, my cousin from Nazareth, stepped into my courtyard and saluted me. Immediately, a great sense of wonder came over me. The baby in my womb turned so quickly, as if he was full of excitement in just hearing Mary's voice. I was no longer just in the presence of a family member – she was divine. I uttered words that I knew were not my own. These were divinely inspired. I was prophesizing. The Holy Spirit came over me, and His power spoke through me: "Blessed are you among women!" Instantly, I knew she, too, was with child. She wasn't showing, she hadn't said anything – I just knew! But, this was not just any ordinary child. This was the Messiah, the promised one, the one Israel had been waiting for so many generations. "Blessed is the fruit of your womb. How is it possible that the mother of my Lord comes to me? As soon as the baby in my womb heard your voice, he leaped for joy!" And I hugged her. I wanted to bow down before her, before her baby. We both could feel the power of the Holy Spirit moving through us. I thanked her for accepting, for having said yes to God. She believed. And through her, will be fulfilled the coming of the Messiah. Prophesies were being fulfilled before our eyes.

We sat down, and we talked and talked for hours. She shared her encounter with the angel Gabriel, the same angel that had visited Zechariah. She shared how wonderful Joseph had been, how worried he was for her before he, too, had his visit from the angel of God in his dream. Her coming to visit me assured her that all that was happening was indeed from God. It also assured me, it was a form of discernment and confirmation of all that had been orchestrated by God. We prayed. Mary started praising God and His goodness in a chant for all to hear:

My soul magnifies the Lord and my spirit rejoices in God my Savior. For he looked with favor on the lowliness of his handmaid and behold henceforth all generations shall call me blessed. For he who is great has done great things for me and holy is his Name. And his mercy is from generation to generation on those who fear him. He has accomplished powerful deeds with his arm. He has scattered the arrogant in the intentions of their heart. He has deposed the powerful from their seat, and he has exalted the humble. He has filled the hungry with good things, and the rich he has sent away empty. He has taken up his servant Israel, mindful of his mercy, just as he spoke to our fathers: to Abraham and to his offspring forever. (Luke 1:46-55)

Mary stayed with me for about three months. She had to return home because any further delay would make her trip back home very difficult walking through the hard terrain through the hillside. Mary wanted to take no chances on the wellbeing of this precious child that had been entrusted to her. And so, at an appointed time, she left. Shortly after her departure, I had my son. What a precious, precious gift. My baby boy! My neighbors and family came to see us as if they expected to see something other than a perfectly healthy baby boy. I couldn't blame their curiosity – I was barren – I was very old! How could it be that I had been blessed with such a perfect baby. Blessed be God!

Zechariah had told me long ago that the angel had told him that our baby was to be called John. I knew people would find it strange that we would name our baby John because no one in our family line, mine or his, had that name. But, God wanted it, God would have it! And so, on the eighth day following John's birth we presented him to the Lord in the temple to be circumcised according to the law. The Rabbi called out the baby's name – Zechariah. Immediately, I yelled out. "Not so, he shall be called John." Everyone was stunned that I had spoken up and then immediately everyone looked to Zechariah. Suddenly, the man who had not spoken in well over nine months, asked for a writing tablet, and while writing down the baby's name, said loudly and clearly – "His name is John!"

I just smiled, for I knew the Holy Spirit was upon us. Everyone was amazed. This is all they could talk about. Everyone wondered who our baby would grow up to be. Everyone was sure he would be used by God for some incredible task. Suddenly, Zechariah started prophesizing, inspired by the Holy Spirit:

Blessed is the Lord God of Israel. For he has visited and has wrought the redemption of his people. And he has raised up a horn of salvation for us, in the house of David his servant, just as he spoke by the mouth of his holy prophets, who are from ages past: salvation from our enemies, and from the hand of all those who hate us, to accomplish mercy with our fathers, and to call to mind his holy testament, the oath, which he swore to Abraham, our father, that he would grant to us, so that having been freed from the hand of our enemies, we may serve him without fear, in holiness and in justice before him, throughout all our days. And you, child, shall be called the prophet of the Most High. For you will go before the face of the Lord: to prepare his ways, to give knowledge of salvation to his people for the remission of their sins, through the heart of the mercy of our God, by which, descending from on high, he has visited us, to illuminate those who sit in darkness and in the shadow of death, and to direct our feet in the way of peace. (Luke 1:68-80)

All who heard were absolutely dumbfounded! This man who has not spoken for months is suddenly prophesizing about our son, who somehow will be called the prophet of the Most High. I just clung to every word he said, and I was sure my little John would play a very important part in God's plan and in preparing the way for our welcoming of our Messiah, the Son of God, the little Jesus my cousin Mary would give birth to. Our John grew and the spirit of God was upon him and he accepted his mission wholeheartedly and prepared himself to be ready for the day when he would be called to prepare the way of the Lord.

What is this telling me?
How does it apply to my life?
What have I learned about Jesus here?

JOSEPH – TO BETHLEHEM

And it happened in those days that a decree went out from Caesar Augustus, so that the whole world would be enrolled. This was the first enrollment; it was made by the ruler of Syria, Quirinius. And all went to be declared, each one to his own city. Then Joseph also ascended from Galilee, from the city of Nazareth, into Judea, to the city of David, which is called Bethlehem, because he was of the house and family of David, in order to be declared, with Mary his espoused wife, who was with child. Then it happened that, while they were there, the days were completed, so that she would give birth. And she brought forth her firstborn son. And she wrapped him in swaddling clothes and laid him in a manger, because there was no room for them at the inn.
(Luke 2:1-7)

Mary returned from visiting her cousin Elizabeth. I had missed her tremendously these three months she was gone. Mary was so excited to tell me all about how Zechariah had been visited by the angel who told him his barren wife was going to have a son; how he didn't believe the angel and was now mute; how Elizabeth was already in her sixth month of her pregnancy, and looked very pregnant. Mary was humbled by Elizabeth's greeting – the words she said, she called her blessed among all women! Only God could have inspired her to say those words. Mary hadn't even told her what had happened to her, Elizabeth didn't even know Mary was with child; yet she knew! Mary was so happy for Elizabeth and Zechariah that they would be having a son. Somehow, Mary knew their son would be involved in our son's life. We didn't exactly know how, since they lived a little far, but their lives would be connected somehow.

When Mary returned from her visit with Elizabeth, everyone could see she was with child! What an amazing sight. I still couldn't believe all that was happening to us! Together we read, re-read, and recited scripture, and all having to do with the coming of the Messiah. All was happening according to plan. Mary now spent her days learning from her mother the things she needed to know about taking care of a baby. She wanted to be the best mother! She wanted to know everything – this was the Son of God that had been entrusted to her, and she needed to take very good care of Him. They spent their days making his little clothing, blankets, and all he would need. Mary learned to make the strips of cloth, called swaddling clothes, to wrap the baby at his birth. Mary said that since I am from the line of David, and Jesus therefore, would also be known as Son of David, she recalled that Solomon, the first son of David, was known for great wisdom and humility (until he turned away from the Lord) and was considered one of the greatest of all the kings of the Earth and that he had said that, although a king, he was born like all others. She began quoting his words:

> And when I was born, I began to breathe the common air, and fell upon the kindred earth, and my first sound was a cry, like that of all. I was nursed with care in swaddling cloths. For no king has had a different beginning of existence; there is for all mankind one entrance into life, and a common departure. Therefore I prayed, and understanding was given me; I called upon God, and the spirit of wisdom came to me. I preferred her to scepters and thrones, and I accounted wealth as nothing in comparison with her. (Solomon 7:3-8)

Mary knew the Messiah would come into this world not among the riches of the world, but His would be a humble birth. This would be a sign that he really is the true Son of David. Like Solomon, before him, Jesus would not be about earthly power and glory.

When Mary was in her last months, a decree was sent out by the ruler of our region Caesar Augustus that everyone had to be enrolled in a census and be taxed accordingly. We had to return to the city of my ancestors to enroll, which meant that Mary and I had to travel to Judea to the city of David, called Bethlehem. My heart sunk when I heard the news. This would be a very difficult trip for Mary. We would have to travel over 90 miles in very difficult terrain. I went to find out about how others were making the journey. We could follow a caravan. We needed the donkey, so at least Mary could ride for a little while, and we could carry some provisions.

I went home to tell Mary. We had to go, but this would be so hard on her. When I got home, Mary already knew; she had heard from the neighbors, and she knew we would have to make the trip to Bethlehem. She smiled. I couldn't understand why she would smile when this was going to be a very difficult journey. Then she said, "All in God's plan." Her faith, her amazing faith, it was just incredible. Then she proceeded to quote from the prophet Micah, *"But you, O Bethlehem, who are too little to be among the clans of Judah, from you shall come forth for me one who is to be ruler in Israel, whose coming forth is from of old, from ancient days."* (Micah 5:2). To Mary, this news was simply confirmation that this was God's plan. She immediately started to prepare what we needed to gather for our journey.

And the day came that we left Nazareth. We left thinking that we would return soon. Mary's mother, Ana, stayed behind, as did most of the people we knew. Mary walked a little bit, then she would ride the donkey, then we would rest a little. Mary never complained. Her face was always radiant and filled with so much joy as she cradled her tummy as if already holding the baby in her arms. She was more worried about me than herself. When she sensed that I was worried about her and the baby, she would simply remind me, "God will take care of us." It took us a little longer than anticipated to travel to Bethlehem. We couldn't travel very far each day and had to rest often because of Mary's condition. When I showed any concern about the trip taking so much longer than we thought, Mary would simply look at me and say, "All in God's plan."

As we were approaching Bethlehem, we could see people coming from everywhere. This little town was so crowded with so many people we could hardly move about. It had been a long time since I had been in Bethlehem, and I didn't know if we still had any relatives in the area. I really didn't know anyone. We needed to find a place to stay. I found a nice shady area and left Mary to rest as I went looking for a place. Everywhere I knocked, there was no room. Everyone I spoke with knew of no place available. I must have been gone for hours. Deflated, I finally decided to return to Mary. When I arrived, Mary could see it in my face that I had no good news. Her face, however, showed no distress. She was concerned, not because we had no place to stay but because the hour was fast approaching. She was going to have the baby. My heart was shattered! What was I going to do? The baby could not be born at a door step. I looked at Mary and again, in her face, I could see a smile coming through. Then I saw a lady step out, I thought she was going to tell us to get out of her property. Instead, Mary introduced me to her and said they had been talking while I was away. This lady felt bad she had no rooms available and could see that Mary was ready to have her baby. Then she said that she had a stable where she kept her animals that we could at least rest and have a roof over our heads. She wouldn't even charge us anything. Without haste, I sat Mary on the donkey, and we went to the stable. When we walked in, there were animals there, and, as if they knew they were in the presence of the Lord, they immediately retreated as to make room for us. They looked at Mary and bowed their heads as if recognizing the presence of a king. I gathered the hay from around the barn and laid Mary down, making her as comfortable as possible. When I realized that

Jesus was going to be born in a stable, I was saddened. How could it be that I could not find a better place for the Messiah to be born? Like all the other times, whenever my heart ached for some iniquity, Mary's look just assured me, "All in God's plan." Let's make the best of it. She fell asleep, and I ran to town to find out what I needed to do for the census. When I returned, Mary was already making ready a place to lay the baby. I searched around the stable and picked up a small wooden box used to put the feed for the animals. I cleaned it up and made a make shift crib for Him. Mary was so pleased with my handy work. She found the crib a perfect place for the baby to lay. I filled it up with the hay that Mary had already gathered. These were certainly humble beginnings.

I stepped outside, and suddenly heard a baby's cry. He is here. I ran inside and I could not believe my eyes, what an incredible sight. Mary was holding our baby. The room was filled with angelic beings adorning the child and Mary. All of heaven's majesty was in this room. The light of God was in this room. I couldn't move. The animals had gathered around the baby and Mary as to cuddle them themselves. I fell to my knees. Emmanuel! God is with us! I bowed down before my baby child – the Son of God. Mary called me to her. She cradled the baby in her arms, and what perfection was this child. She looked at me and said, "He is on loan to us, to care for, to love, to support, and to make ready the plans of God." Then she gave me the baby child to hold. There was no greater joy felt by anyone in this world, except perhaps Mary. The angelic beings surrounding us began singing canticles of joy and peace which filled our hearts and overpowered our souls.

What is this telling me?
How does it apply to my life?
What have I learned about Jesus here?

THE STAR

And so, when Jesus had been born in Bethlehem of Judah, in the days of king Herod, behold, Magi from the east arrived in Jerusalem, saying: Where is he who was born king of the Jews? For we have seen his star in the east, and we have come to adore him... Then, seeing the star, they were gladdened by a very great joy. (Mathew 2:1-2 and 2:10)

I am way up in the heavens. I am not the smallest of stars, but I am not the biggest of stars among these gazillions majesties in the sky. Something was happening. There was so much excitement in the air. Angels were abound everywhere, and there were so many coming towards me. What a great spectacle. Something incredible was about to happen. I could just feel it. Then, I was surrounded by a host of angels. I had a mission. God was assigning me to be part of this incredible plan. God, our creator, was revealing His majestic plan for humanity. The little planet Earth was being graced with God's presence. His Son was going to live among them. Earth, a little speck of dirt in the sky, was going to receive God personified. The angels with all of their might began to pull me closer to Earth. My glow was so bright that neither the Earth nor the sky could miss my presence. I was a phenomenon. Learned men had studied for centuries about this event, scriptures foretold of this great event, many had prophesied about it, and many have been expecting it for years – a sign in the sky foretelling the birth of a new king, and I, I was that sign. But, not only was I the sign, I was going to guide kings and their emissaries to find the new child king.

I could see lands far away from each other, on planet Earth, people fixated on my light. They pointed, they wondered what exactly they were seeing. Soon multitudes of people and their caravans began traveling. I showed them the way, where to go. People from different lands, and after many months, they came together in the middle of the desert. There was lots of pointing at my bright light, and their faces were filled with joy just realizing that others were following me. Everyone knew something extraordinary was happening. I led them with my light that, although brighter than the sun would not burn them. They were led through the desert comfortably. All walked for many months to get to Judea. The angels were the force behind me, they knew the way, and we all followed. The angels guided me, and I guided the people to a little town called Bethlehem of Judea.

The leaders of the caravans stopped to introduce themselves to the king of Judea, who was King Herod at the time. It is customary that those formal introductions be made, and although they knew where they were headed and had me guiding them for all those months, they could not contain their excitement and told Herod that they had seen me in the sky who brought them here to pay homage to the new King of the Jews who would be born in the little town of Bethlehem as had been prophesied by many a prophet. I continued on and came to rest above the place where baby Jesus, his mother Mary and Joseph were living.

Just like that, once my assignment was complete, I retrieved to my place in the universe!

What is this telling me?
How does it apply to my life?
What have I learned about Jesus here?

THE SHEPHERDS

And there were shepherds in the same region, being vigilant and keeping watch in the night over their flock. And behold, an Angel of the Lord stood near them, and the brightness of God shone around them, and they were struck with a great fear. And the Angel said to them: "Do not be afraid. For behold, I proclaim to you a great joy, which will be for all the people. For today a Savior has been born for you in the city of David: he is Christ the Lord. And this will be a sign for you: you will find the infant wrapped in swaddling clothes and lying in a manger." And suddenly there was with the Angel a multitude of the celestial army, praising God and saying: "Glory to God in the highest, and on earth peace to men of good will." And it happened that, when the Angel had departed from them into heaven, the shepherds said to one another, "Let us cross over to Bethlehem and see this word, which has happened, which the Lord has revealed to us. And they went quickly. And they found Mary and Joseph; and the infant was lying in a manger. Then, upon seeing this, they understood the word that had been spoken to them about this boy. And all who heard it were amazed by this, and by those things which were told to them by the shepherds. But Mary kept all these words, pondering them in her heart. And the shepherds returned, glorifying and praising God for all the things that they had heard and seen, just as it was told to them. (Luke 2:8-20)

I was watching over our flock with my father, and we were absolutely amazed by the brightness of this shining star that seemed to hover over Bethlehem. We had never seen anything like it before. Even though it was night, we could see clearly as day. Other shepherds in the region were baffled at the sight as well, wondering what it could mean. A group of us had gathered together, looking at the star still wondering. Suddenly, it was as if the light of the star came towards us and engulfed us in this most beautiful light. A beautiful being appeared before our eyes. We looked at each other to make sure everyone was seeing the same thing. Everyone was simply amazed. We couldn't believe our eyes. We didn't know what this could mean. We were all afraid for ourselves, for our flock, and for everyone. This was an angel of God, we just knew it. I had never heard of anything like this happening to anyone, but I knew I was in the presence of God's messengers. We were in the presence of angels. Then, as if the angel could read our thoughts, he said, "Do not be afraid. For behold, I proclaim to you a great joy, which will be for all the people. For today a Savior has been born for you in the city of David: he is Christ the Lord. And this will be a sign for you: you will find the infant wrapped in swaddling clothes and lying in a manger." As soon as he finished proclaiming this amazing news, suddenly there was a multitude of the most beautiful celestial beings, and they started praising God and singing in the most angelic of voices saying, "Glory to God in the highest, and on Earth peace to men of good will." And just as quickly as they came, they disappeared. We all looked at each other, to make sure that our eyes had not deceived us. We all had just witnessed the most beautiful of visions. We had been invited to meet Christ the Lord! Some of the shepherds were not of Jewish decent, and so they were not well versed in the prophesies of old telling us that God would be sending a savior, so we explained it to them. But the angel told us that he was proclaiming a great joy for all people. Everyone! We, these lowly shepherds, tending our flocks as we did everyday, have been chosen by God, through this angelic message, to welcome the Messiah, to visit Him first, and to tell everyone that He was now among us! Each one of us grabbed our very best sheep and crossed over to Bethlehem, to the place marked by the star, and surely as it was proclaimed by the angel, we found the child laying in a manger, wrapped in swaddling clothes, while his mother and father sat in adoration of Him. We knew we were before a king. We bowed, we adored, we offered our gifts, and our eyes had never seen a more beautiful sight!

We all returned home, each to different sections of the region. All we could do was glorify and praise God for all the things that we had heard and seen, just as it was told to us by the angel of the Lord.

What is this telling me?
How does it apply to my life?
What have I learned about Jesus here?

SIMEON

*And after eight days were ended, so that the boy would be cir-
cumcised, his name was called JESUS, just as he was called by
the Angel before he was conceived in the womb. And after the
days of her purification were fulfilled, according to the law of
Moses, they brought him to Jerusalem, in order to present him
to the Lord, just as it is written in the law of the Lord, "for every
male opening the womb shall be called holy to the Lord," and
in order to offer a sacrifice, according to what is said in the law
of the Lord, "a pair of turtledoves or two young pigeons." And
behold, there was a man in Jerusalem, whose name was Simeon,
and this man was just and God-fearing, awaiting the consolation
of Israel. And the Holy Spirit was with him. And he had received
an answer from the Holy Spirit: that he would not see his own
death before he had seen the Christ of the Lord. And, he went
with the Spirit to the temple. And when the child Jesus was
brought in by his parents, in order to act on his behalf according
to the custom of the law, he also took him up, into his arms, and
he blessed God and said: "Now you may dismiss your servant
in peace, O Lord, according to your word. For my eyes have seen
your salvation, which you have prepared before the face of all
people: the light of revelation to the nations and the glory of your
people Israel." And his father and mother were wondering over
these things, which were spoken about him. And Simeon blessed
them, and he said to his mother Mary: "Behold, this one has
been set for the ruin and for the resurrection of many in Israel,
and as a sign which will be contradicted. And a sword will pass
through your own soul, so that the thoughts of many hearts may
be revealed." And there was a prophetess, Anna, a daughter of
Phanuel, from the tribe of Asher. She was very advanced in years,
and she had lived with her husband for seven years from her vir-
ginity. And then she was a widow, even to her eighty-fourth year.*

And without departing from the temple, she was a servant to fasting and prayer, night and day. And entering at the same hour, she confessed to the Lord. And she spoke about him to all who were awaiting the redemption of Israel. (Luke 2:21-38)

I am an old man. I am a man of God. I come to the temple every day, but in the last few years, after dedicating my prayers to the Lord, I tend to sit at the temple gates, waiting in anticipation for the fulfillment of the promise of God. I want to be the first to greet Him when He comes to the temple. In my youth, I received a revelation from God that I would not die before seeing the prophesy of the Messiah fulfilled. My very eyes would see the savior of our people Israel.

I am well versed in all the prophesies surrounding the coming of the Messiah. I know the time is near. I saw the great sign in the sky. I heard about the bright brilliant star hovering above Bethlehem. I heard that lowly shepherds were invited to greet the baby. Keeping with tradition according to the law of Moses, eight days after his birth, his parents will soon bring him to the temple to be consecrated to God. I waited anxiously.

Then one day, as I was about to take my seat by the temple gates, I saw a young couple approaching. The spirit within me was stirred up. It was them. It had to be them. How young was that mother holding her baby boy in her arms. I ran to them. I know I startled them. I could not contain my excitement. I almost ripped the baby from her arms and lifted him up in prayer thanking God that His promise had been fulfilled. People were gathering around us, and I simply uttered my praise to the Lord, thanking Him that the day was upon us. I told God, He could take me now, I could die in peace, "for my eyes had seen your salvation, which you have prepared before the face of all peoples: the light of revelation to the nations and the glory of your people Israel." Mary and Joseph looked at each other, wondering what was happening; wondering who I was and why I would be making such a scene. But they could feel that the Spirit of God was with me. I heard Mary tell Joseph, "All in God's plan." I blessed them and thanked God for their willingness to accept God's will to allow God's plan to unfold before our eyes. After I had blessed them, I looked at His mother and said, "Behold, your son has been set for the ruin and for the resurrection of many in Israel, and as a sign which will be contradicted." Mary seemed a little confused, not fully understanding my words. Suddenly enlightened, she knew there would be many who would not believe in her Son and His message, would not accept that He was the long awaited savior, and she understood full well that there would be many for generations to come who would gain their salvation through Him. Then, my heart ached, and the pain and suffering I felt deep in my soul was not my own. This pain was for this young mother – the mother of our Savior. I looked at her, and the spirit of God worked through me and I told her, "A sword will pierce through your very soul…" Mary knew the meaning of this message fully well, and she cradled her baby boy, kissing his little head and cuddling His little body wanting to protect Him from all harm. She knew His mission in life would not be easy, but she was going to be with Him every step of the way – for whatever and however God needed her – God is in control and whatever was to happen to Him and to them, it was all, in God's plan.

Suddenly, as if to offer more proof to all who were around us, the prophetess Anna was heard to prophesy that this baby was the long-awaited redeemer of Israel. Anna was well regarded in the community. She was a widow for many years, and she was now very aged. After she lost her husband, she dedicated herself to the Lord. She was a woman of prayer and fasting, night a day. She re-affirmed my message for all to hear. The savior of the world, the long-awaited redeemer of the world was among us on this day, right now.

What is this telling me?
How does it apply to my life?
What have I learned about Jesus here?

THE MAGI

And so, when Jesus had been born in Bethlehem of Judah, in the days of king Herod, behold, Magi from the east arrived in Jerusalem, saying: "Where is he who was born king of the Jews? For we have seen his star in the east, and we have come to adore him..." Then, Herod, quietly calling the Magi, diligently learned from them the time when the star appeared to them. And sending them into Bethlehem, he said: "Go and diligently ask questions about the boy. And when you have found him, report back to me, so that I too, may come and adore him." And when they had heard the king, they went away. And behold, the star that they had seen in the east went before them, even until, arriving, it stood still above the place where the child was. Then, seeing the star, they were gladdened by a very great joy. And entering the home, they found the boy with his Mother. And so, falling prostrate, they adored him. And opening their treasures, they offered him gifts: gold, frankincense and myrrh. And having received a response in sleep that they should not return to Herod, they went back by another way to their own region. (Matthew 2:1-2; 7-12)

I am Baltazar. I have always been fascinated by the stars. I have studied the stars for many years, and every so often many learned men from different nations would meet and astronomers talked about a great mystery that is about to enfold having to do with the stars. We don't know when it's going to happen' and it will proclaim something incredible orchestrated by God, the Creator of the universe. And so today I feel that sign is upon us, and the sign is a great star that just appeared in the heavens. It is bright and shinier than all the stars in the heavens. It is brighter than the sun. It's such a rare occurrence that it must be what we have been waiting for. I have to get ready, ready to meet the rest of the leaders who I am sure will also be compelled to travel a far to find this king, to find the one who is going to be the king of the Jews. I gathered my servants, as we had been prepared for so many years, all the camels, the provisions and the manpower we needed to travel to Judea. Our journey will take many months to get to our destination. This event in the sky, this incredible light, would guide us there.

When the day came, I left my throne to others and left on a journey I wasn't sure I would ever come back from, but this journey, I had to make. Because I was going to find a king, the King of the Jews, another king, I needed to take a gift. I chose frankincense because this holy child was going to be a holy man of God. I hoped my counter-parts had seen the same sign in the sky and they were also preparing themselves.

I am Melchior. I saw the light, I saw the star, and I have to go. I just need to go. I gathered my caravan, I checked my charts, and I have no doubt that this is the sign we have been waiting for. The incredible massive event was enfolding. I asked my people to gather the gold I had been storing for this moment. It is my most precious and valuable material possession. A piece of gold worthy for royalty, a king. This was my offering. I was going to take gold to offer Him. I can't wait to get to where we are being led.

I am a devout Jew. I have dedicated my life to studying scripture. I know what has been foretold of the Messiah to come to liberate our people, the new King of the Jews! All the chief priests and devout people of my kingdom know the scriptures, we know very well about the prophesies about the coming of the Messiah. We all await Him with great anticipation. I am a learned man. Not only have I devoted my life to studying and praying the scriptures, but because of them, I have also devoted my life to studying the stars. There are several others like me.

I am Gaspar, from the land of Persia. I know the kings from Arabia and the land of Sheba have also devoted their lives to studying the stars, preparing for the coming of the Lord as it has been prophesied. My caravan is ready. At a moment's notice, I can go and find the new king of the Jews. I have all the men and provisions necessary to make the long journey to the land of Judea. I went to my prayer room and took out the gift I have saved all these years to give to the Messiah. It will take us many, many months to travel across the desert to get there, but I am ready, and I know others are as well. We, the students of the stars, have all felt the time was approaching that in our life time we would welcome the Messiah, the new king of the Jews.

As I sat deep in thought and prayer with all my maps laid out before me, contemplating all the marvelous things in this world, I had an uncanny feeling that I was about to experience something absolutely incredible. Suddenly, one of my servants entered the room in haste. He told me to look out the window because there was something very strange in the sky. There was an event in the sky that will undoubtably confirm all our suspicions. My servant tells me the sign is in the sky. As I stepped to the window and open it, I looked over to the east, and there it was – a magnificent star in the heavens. My whole body felt such tremendous peace, tremendous joy, and I just knew I was about to witness and experience the most wonderful event in history. The star was so bright and so close to the Earth I thought I could touch it. My whole body trembled, and I was overcome with a great sense of awe. There was no doubt in my mind that this was the sign we had been waiting for. I was convinced my counter-parts were witnessing the same thing. I needed to summon my people and give them the great news. I needed to set my caravan in motion. It was time to go. I am sure we will meet others along the way.

Without haste, I gathered all the people I had assigned who would be making this journey with me. I know there would be others to share this great event, and so we must go. I went and picked up the gift that I needed to present to the new king. My gift is myrrh. Myrrh is an incredible spice. I didn't quite understand why I picked myrrh, as it is associated with suffering, but I really felt this was the gift God wanted me to present to the new king.

As we started on our way it was as if the brilliant star just hovered over our caravan giving us enough light that we were able to travel during the night and avoiding the scorching sun during the day. We traveled many months not sure where the star would lead us. Many people got discouraged along the way and probably even thought I must be mad. Until, suddenly, as if a mirage appeared before our eyes, we could see other caravans approaching. This surely gave life to us all. This surely was confirmation that the prophesy would be filled. We rested awhile, and I met Melchior from the land of Arabia and Baltazar from Sheba. We got together to pray and to share our thoughts. We were all convinced the star was leading us to Bethlehem of Judea. They, too, were led by the star ahead of them who brought us all together. Only God could have orchestrated such perfection and guided us here.

Both Melchior and Baltazar shared how they saw the star in the East and felt compelled to get ready their caravans and go to Judea. Both were men of great faith. We were all amazed, but not surprised, we had found each other here in the desert looking for the same king. Months and months traveling through the desert, our hearts were bursting with anticipation of what we might find in Bethlehem. From our calculations, the child would have been born already.

As we approached Judea, we began inquiring about the birth of the new king of the Jews. It was as though we were speaking a foreign language. This incredible event happening right here, and no one was talking about it or they were too scared to speak. A shepherd's son heard us asking about the new born child, and he shared how he and his father were in the fields tending their flocks when right above them, coming from the sky, a majestic choir of angels appeared, telling them to go to a nearby stable where animals were kept because a child of God had been born. They immediately left and encountered others on the way, and they went and found everything just as the angels had told them. Other shepherds and people kept coming and saw the same thing.

The word was spreading that we the kings from faraway lands were inquiring about the birth of the new King of the Jews. Soon, King Herod, the king of that region summoned us to his palace as a gesture of good will welcoming us to his land. The king seemed keenly interested in what the people were talking about around town. He was already well informed about the anticipated birth of the new king of the Jews. He asked us where this king would be born and said that he, too, wanted to pay him homage.

As we started out of the palace the three of us felt very uneasy with King Herod's interest about the child. There seemed something very sinister about Herod's inquiry. Another thing that was extremely curious is that the bright star in the sky was such an incredible phenomenon that could not be ignored. Yet, Herod and his court seemed oblivious to it, it was as if they could not see it. We looked up, to make sure it was still there. We noticed the star was ahead of us with its light brightly glowing over a small building. It was over the town of Bethlehem just as it had been prophesied. We set out to find it. Many followed us. The light concentrated and covered a small modest home. We knocked. The door was opened, and we entered it. They always welcomed all who came to see the baby. There, walking towards us was a most beautiful girl with her baby in her arms. We all fell to our knees in adoration. We could not speak. The spirit of God came upon us. God was truly among us!

Then, one by one, we uncovered our precious gifts for the baby child. Baltazar offered frankincense, the fragrance of divinity, a gift for a holy man, a prayer offering. Melchior offered gold, a gift fit for a royal king. I offered myrrh, a spice associated with suffering and death, for I felt this child would suffer much to save his people. We adored Him and blessed Him. We had witnessed the coming of our king, the savior of all people. Our mission in life felt complete.

We set up camp and prepared to rest before returning to our homes. In the evening, we three kings met for prayer and reflection on all that we had witnessed. We were truly blessed! Suddenly, we were in the presence of a holy angel of God. He confirmed the child we had just paid homage to was indeed the new king of the Jews of whom had been prophesied in our holy books. He also instructed us not to return to Herod, for Herod wanted to know about the child to kill him. Without haste, we dismantled our tents and started out of Judea without returning to Herod.

What is this telling me?
How does it apply to my life?
What have I learned about Jesus here?

JOSEPH – TO EGYPT

And after they had gone away, behold, an Angel of the Lord appeared in a dream to Joseph, saying: "Rise up, and take the boy and his mother and flee into Egypt. And remain there until I tell you. For it will happen that Herod will seek the boy to destroy him." And getting up, he took the boy and his mother by night, and withdrew into Egypt. And he remained there, until the death of Herod, in order to fulfill what was spoken by the Lord through the prophet, saying: "Out of Egypt, I called my son." (Matthew 2:13- 15)

Mary and I had settled in well, in Bethlehem. We thought we could stay here awhile. Every day, people were stopping by to see the baby, and he was growing stronger every day. We could see it in all of their faces; either they believed and relished what they were witnessing or didn't see anything special or different with this baby, and we, the parents, just looked too ordinary. Some were just indifferent. All these months, Mary and I kept reliving all the wonderful things that had happened since the birth of Jesus. The shepherds coming, sharing they were instructed by the angels of God to visit the baby and finding Him just as the angels told them. They couldn't hold their excitement. The visit of the Magi and their beautiful gifts. We were honored and humbled with their presence. They told us how they had studied the stars and studied the scriptures handed down by our ancestors. They had no doubt Jesus was the Savior of the world, which fulfilled the prophesies of so many centuries ago. We talked about our visit to the temple and our encounter with old man Simeon. When Mary thought about Simeon's words that a sword would pierce her soul, she knew Jesus would suffer so much that her soul would hurt, and she wouldn't be able to help Him. Her heart ached when she tried to imagine what could happen to Him, but we couldn't imagine. All in God's plan were her famous words of confidence!

Some of the people who came to visit us started saying some of King Herod's men had been asking about the baby. Apparently, King Herod also wanted to meet Jesus. The Magi had told us as much although we found it strange that the Magi didn't come back to see us again. We heard their caravans had picked up and left in the middle of the night.

We had had a full day and went to bed early. Suddenly, in the middle of the night, I had a dream. It was the angel of God, the same angel that had visited me before. He told me to get up immediately, to take Mary and the baby and go to the land of Egypt and to remain there until he returns with further instructions. The angel said that we needed to leave right away because King Herod was looking for us to kill our baby. Without hesitation, I did as the angel instructed me to do. I woke up Mary, and we gathered what we could for our journey. I didn't know how to go to Egypt, but I knew I had to get a guide to take us there. And, divinely organized, we found someone who would take us to Egypt. Mary and I were so thankful we had the gift of gold given to us by one of the Magi. We could use that to pay the guide to take us all the way to Egypt. It would pay for our food, for the setting up our tent along the way, and for our guide's wages. It would certainly take months to reach Egypt traveling with a baby, but we felt better that we had someone traveling with us. This was completely foreign territory to us, and Mary was convinced the guide was an angel sent to us from God. I had no reason to question her.

I wondered why God would have us flee to Egypt. Mary reminded me that God had led Moses and His people out of Egypt and he was now leading us into Egypt until an appointed time when he would call us out of Egypt. And she quoted scripture that said "out of Egypt I called my Son!" (Hosea 11:1)

> *What is this telling me?*
> *How does it apply to my life?*
> *What have I learned about Jesus here?*

HEROD

Then Herod, seeing that he had been fooled by the Magi, was very angry. And so he sent to kill all the boys who were in Bethlehem, and in all its borders, from two years of age and under, according to the time that he had learned by questioning the Magi. Then what was spoken through the prophet Jeremiah was fulfilled, saying: "A voice has been heard in Ramah, great weeping and wailing. Rachel crying for her sons. And she was not willing to be consoled, because they were no more." (Matthew 2:16-18)

I just heard that the three kings who I invited into my home and welcomed to partake in a meal together have left our region without coming back to me to tell me where the child was, the so-called new King of the Jews. They were very ungrateful. I treated them so well. Why would they leave without telling me what I had instructed them to do? There is no other king in this place but me! What am I to do now? I've already summoned all the religious leaders in this region, and no one knows where the child is. They know where He was born, but they don't know where He is now! Are they lying to me? People claim they don't know who He is. Some knew the parents but said they had moved shortly after they were visited by the kings. Some would say they lived in one side of town while others would say another side of town. There was some talk that He was born in a stable. I had my men look for them everywhere. Would a king really choose to be born in a stable? He can't be much of a king! But why do I feel so threatened by this baby king? Will He entice people to revolt against me? I am the only king here, I must find this new king of the Jews and deal with Him right away.

I was getting more and more upset as the reports kept coming to me that no one knew where to find this child. I started hearing rumors that His parents had already fled the region, but no one could tell me where they had gone or where they were going. I have spent weeks looking for one single child. I had had enough! I summoned my guards and gave strict orders that all male children under the age of two years old were to be killed. Jew, gentile, Greek, it did not matter. Perhaps if the parents heard what I was about to do, they would reveal themselves. But nothing happened. I was furious. So, I gave my soldiers a new order, they were to kill not just the children in Bethlehem, but extend to all neighboring borders. My soldiers looked at me as if they had not heard my orders correctly or rather as if they did not want to hear what I was saying. I sent them on their way, and they were to follow my orders immediately. Shortly after they left, I could hear screams and cries and pleas from the women. Babies crying then going silent. I was winning this battle. I felt vindicated that the kings had not obeyed me, and I felt victory over the King of the Jews who had tried to evade me. He would be dead, I was sure. And so, the cries and lamentations continued for days. The streets were covered with the bodies of slaughtered babies and the mothers who dared to defy me and tried to save their babies. Those mothers who survived wished they had died because there was no consolation to their pain. Day after day, I could hear those cries. I hated to go to sleep because I had nightmares of the slaughtering of all those innocent babies. In my dreams, I was a soldier killing them without pity. Day after day, I was tormented with the cries coming from everywhere. When I was awake, there were infinite reminders of what I had done, and I found no peace. I was tormented with the sites and the sounds all around me. Worst of all no one could assure me that the child who was to be king of the Jews had died. Had He escaped? Would He grow up to take over my kingdom? He must have died!

What is this telling me?
How does it apply to my life?
What have I learned about Jesus here?

MARY – FROM EGYPT

Then, when Herod had passed away, behold, an Angel of the Lord appeared in a dream to Joseph in Egypt, saying: "Rise up, and take the boy and his mother, and go into the land of Israel. For those who were seeking the life of the boy have passed away." And rising up, he took the boy and his mother, and he went into the land of Israel. Then, hearing that Archelaus reigned in Judea in place of his father Herod, he was afraid to go there. And being warned in sleep, he withdrew into parts of Galilee. And arriving, he lived in a city which is called Nazareth, in order to fulfill what was spoken through the prophets: "For he shall be called a Nazarene."
(Matthew 2:19-23)

Many years passed, and our boy grew strong. Jesus loved life. He loved working with Joseph, helping him and learning to work with the wood. Together, they would make so many beautiful things. Many times, I would catch Jesus just looking at the planks of wood as if He knew their purpose and how they connected to Him. I didn't interrupt His thoughts, but I wondered.

Jesus' favorite time of the day was to read scripture. He wanted to know everything that had been written in our books, and He did. Sometimes when we were in prayer, He would explain scripture with such simplicity and authority that it truly touched our hearts. His enlightenment about God, creation and the human race was incredible. Sometimes Joseph and I would ask each other – how and where did He learn all these beautiful things? And immediately, we knew, the Holy Spirit was upon Him, there was no denying. He had the best of all teachers, and He heeded His instructions. Jesus was so human, that sometimes we forgot He was the Son of God. Jesus was so full of wisdom and all could see that the grace of God was with Him. Jesus was so loving and so giving to all that it was infectious. We all wanted to imitate him.

Life was a little hard, living in Egypt where the reminders of our ancestors' pain and suffering was everywhere, especially in the massive buildings. Jesus reflected often on those days, when Joseph (centuries ago), who was betrayed by his own brothers, had become a ruler of Egypt. Joseph triumphed over hatred because his love for God was immense and his faith in God's will for his life was unshakeable. Jesus reminded us that Moses was called to lead our people out of Egypt and would add that, we, too, would be called to leave Egypt; this would be a temporary stay for us. All in God's plan kept coming to mind. Joseph and I just marveled at the presence of Jesus, and our hearts swelled with joy.

And, as we had been expecting for many years, Joseph was again told in a dream that King Herod had died, and we could return to Israel. We made the long journey back, but when we heard that Herod's son, Archelaus, reigned in his place, we felt compelled to return to our home in Nazareth. Suddenly, under my breath, I found myself quoting scripture, saying, "he shall be called a Nazarene!"

> *What is this telling me?*
> *How does it apply to my life?*
> *What have I learned about Jesus here?*

MARY – THE FINDING IN THE TEMPLE

And after they had performed all things according to the law of the Lord, they returned to Galilee, to their city, Nazareth. Now the child grew, and he was strengthen with the fullness of wisdom. And the grace of God was in him. And his parents went every year to Jerusalem, at the time of the solemnity of Passover. And when he had become twelve years old, they ascended to Jerusalem, according to the custom of the feast day. And having completed the days, when they returned, the boy Jesus remained in Jerusalem. And his parents did not realize this. But, supposing that he was in the company, they went a day's journey, seeking him among their relatives and acquaintances. And not finding him, they returned to Jerusalem, seeking him. And it happened that, after three days, they found him in the temple, sitting in the midst of the doctors, listening to them and questioning them. But all who listened to him were astonished over his prudence and his responses. And upon seeing him, they wondered. And his mother said to him: "Son, why have you acted this way towards us? Behold, your father and I were seeking you in sorrow. And he said to them: How is it that you were seeking me? For did you not know that it is necessary for me to be in these things which are of my Father? And they did not understand the word that he spoke to them. And he descended with them and went to Nazareth. And he was subordinate to them. And his mother kept all these words in her heart. And Jesus advanced in wisdom and in age and in grace, with God and men. (Luke 2:39-52)

Every year we traveled to Jerusalem to celebrate the feast of the Passover. This one year, when Jesus was 12 years old, we celebrated and made our offerings, and once the caravan got ready to return to

Nazareth, Joseph and I gathered everything. Jesus had gone to the temple and was now playing with His friends before we got underway. As we started our journey, we asked some of our family and friends if they had seen Jesus. We were assured He was ahead of us. We started walking a little faster than most trying to find Jesus. I sent word that whoever saw Him to please send Him our way.

As the day came to an end, we never heard from Jesus. This was very unlike Him, to not let us know where He was. Some acquaintances told us that He was well behind us and He was okay. We waited and waited. Jesus never caught up with us, and we had made our way up to the front of the pack. We were about a day and a half into the trip when I told Joseph I could not continue another step without seeing Jesus. He was lost, and we needed to find Him. Joseph tried to calm me down, but I could see he, too, was worried. We decided that we should return back to Jerusalem if we had to, but we had to find Jesus. We kept searching and started to make our way back to the end of the pack, and we were asking everyone we passed if they had seen Jesus, but no one knew anything. Some told us that they had seen him last in Jerusalem. We were frantic. My heart was beating a thousand beats a minute. I prayed and perhaps my fear overpowered my thoughts – I had lost my son! Had someone taken him? Was he hurt? We pressed on and finally arrived in Jerusalem. Our first instinct was to search the temple. Jesus loves His prayer time; perhaps He couldn't find us and was praying that we come back to him. We entered the temple, and we heard His voice. I recognized that sweet beautiful voice. I grabbed Joseph's hand and hurried towards the voice. Then, I slowed down my steps, I not only wanted to hear that sweet soothing voice, but I also wanted to hear what He was saying. As I approached the prayer area, I could see Him from behind the wooden window – He was asking questions to the elders and challenging them on the meaning of the scriptures. Elders were asking Him questions and all were amazed at His answers. How could so much wisdom come out of this child? How could He be so well versed in scripture and its meaning? What kind of questions were these that He was asking that baffled the elders? My heart was at peace that we found Him, and we let Him continue with His prayer and sharing. When done, we approached Him. I couldn't contain my anxiety and pain of not knowing where He had been. My fear and reproach got the best of me. I asked Him how He could have scared us, His father and I, in such a way? He seemed puzzled at my questioning but almost realizing that He knew the time had not yet come for Joseph and I to understand what had just happened, He looked at me and said, "Did you not know I must be in Father's house?" Immediately, I was reminded what I had told Joseph long ago – He is on loan to us; to love and support. It was clear His father was our Father in heaven. He was here on a mission, and He was very much aware of where He belonged.

On the way home, we talked and Jesus shared with Joseph and I all that He had done in the temple, and it troubled Him greatly how the hearts of so many religious leaders had departed from God.

What is this telling me?
How does it apply to my life?
What have I learned about Jesus here?

THE DONKEY

I was in a small patch of grass. I was just lying there. I felt very weak, and I had no strength to even look for food. My master had sent me away because I got a little sick, and I was no longer able to do the very hard work he had me doing for so many years. I was very strong then. I was my master's pride and joy and the envy of many. But, when I got sick, my owner had no need for me and just sent me away. You could say I am homeless. I have been trotting aimlessly, but I am getting weaker and weaker. Even laying down to rest is cumbersome. My bones hurt when I touch the ground and trying to get up takes all my strength, but I have to do it. I have to find some food. Much of what is around me, I have eaten to the bare roots. I need to move even if a little bit and get some food.

As I stood up, I heard a noise. I see someone. I wanted to just go away, but I have no strength to run away and maybe if I just lay down quietly, he won't see me. And just as I thought about how I was going to let myself down, without causing too much pain, I froze. The man was right in front of me. He had a piece of wood on one hand. I feared for my life. Was he going to use that piece of wood to hit me and send me away? If I could, I would just go away, and he wouldn't need to hit me. I lowered my head as if I was preparing for the beating to begin, but instead, I see him extending his other arm. I couldn't believe it; on his other hand he has some straw. He was walking towards me so gently as if to tell me not to be afraid. He kept motioning his hand with the straw. He wanted me to eat it. He is trying to feed me! I still couldn't move, but he got close enough that just smelling that straw gave me new life. I ate. He left. I wanted to tell him not to leave, but I was too busy enjoying this little bit of food. I hear him again. Then I see he is coming towards me again, and this time he has a bunch of straw in his hands. I fell to the ground. I had enough straw to sustain me for days. I had a friend. He just looked at me eating, and I think he was as happy watching me as I was eating. He is a good man. Then he left. I was sad, but I couldn't believe I could just stay here, eat my straw, and try to regain some strength. What a glorious day this was.

The next day, about the same time, I see the man coming at a distance. I see he was picking up pieces of wood and laying them down to the side. He would pick up a piece, look at it, as if in his mind he was creating a masterpiece. I watched. My belly was full, and I had slept well. I mustered enough energy to walk towards him. He seemed glad to see me. He reached out his hand, and I allowed it to touch my body. The stroke of his hand healed my bones. I felt strong in an instant. I was energized. I felt no pain! I did feel some hesitation on his part as he touched my skeletal frame, but I wanted to make sure he knew his touch was welcome. I kept trotting beside him, and I kept following him as he continued to pick up the wooden pieces. He had a whole pile already. He started to pile up some pieces of wood on a piece of cloth and put them on his shoulders. He was carrying them home. Oh, I wanted to tell him to load them up on me, I could carry them for him. But I didn't, and he left. I felt compelled to remain near the pile of wood he left behind. I was guarding it for him. He would be back for them, and I would see him again. And so it was that a few days later, he came. He searched for more wood, and I was right there with him. He was happy to see I looked rejuvenated. I was hopping around, and I wanted to tell him to use me to carry his wood. I must have been really convincing that suddenly I feel a nice thick blanket over my body. He placed the pieces of wood on it, and I was so happy. I was going to be useful again. He loaded me up and kept looking at me as if to ask me if it was okay. It was perfectly fine. Then, he led me to his home. He fed me, and I really didn't want to leave. I was home. I was hoping he would let me stay. I laid down quietly, and for the first time in a long time, I slept profoundly, with no worries.

In the days that followed, I got to meet Mary, the most wonderful of people. She would always make sure I had enough to eat, she wanted to make sure I was alright. I would go with Joseph to pick up wood, and he made some beautiful things with them. He even made one that looked like me and gave it to Mary. I was so very honored.

One day, Joseph came to me and said he needed me to go on a very important assignment. He wasn't going with us, but Mary needed to travel to the hillside of Judea to see some relatives. I was very excited. He loaded me up, and we got under way. We joined a caravan going there, and we felt safe. This was a difficult trip, but Mary never complained. She always had a smile on her face, and there was not a worry that would shake her existence. It was as if she was sure everything would work out fine. God was in control and whatever came her way, it was well orchestrated by God. When we got to the home of Zechariah and Elizabeth, we were received almost like royalty. I was very well taken care of. Mary would still come every day and make sure I was well fed and rested. We stayed there for some time and then returned back to Joseph. We were very happy to see Joseph. But, something very exciting was happening because Mary couldn't stop talking about all that was happening with Elizabeth, and all Joseph would say was, "Praise God."

My family, my new owners, were the best of humans, and I was happy to see the family was growing! Life went back to normal for a few months until one day Joseph came home very sad. I heard something about how glad they were to have me (me, the donkey) because I was going to make the journey a little easier. We were going on another journey, and this time we were all going! This must be something very important because there were many people in the town who were preparing for this trip. Then Joseph came to me and said I had another very important assignment. It was going to be longer than the trip to the hillside, and because Mary was with child,

I was going to carry her along the way. I was ready for this assignment. I was very excited about this new assignment. I was going to help Mary and her baby. I needed nothing else! There were many animals going on this trip. I could see Joseph was very concerned about Mary doing the trip because she was already in her last months of her pregnancy. But, Mary was always able to wipe out all those concerns away when he spoke with her.

And so the day came, we joined an enormous caravan and headed to Judea, to a little town called Bethlehem. Joseph's relatives were from there. It took us months to get there. The roads were treacherous, the weather was harsh, and there was some discord among some people but my masters, they were the best. I was happiest when I carried Mary on my back. There was so much peace radiating from her. I never felt any pain when I carried her, on the contrary, I felt like I was treading on air, like another force was carrying us. I felt so strong, I felt invincible! This little baby Mary was carrying was someone special, I could feel it.

As we approached Bethlehem, we could see caravans coming from everywhere. The little town was too little for all these people. There were tents pitched along the road for miles away. Joseph wanted to get closer to the town because he felt Mary was going to give birth very soon. Joseph left Mary and I resting in the town, and he left to try and find a room. It didn't seem like there was anything available any more. Mary was talking to the home owner where she was sitting and she seemed to have offered some suggestion. Mary looked so peaceful. Joseph had been gone quite a while already. When Joseph returned to us, we could see the sadness all over his face. There was nothing available; he didn't know what to do. I wanted to tell him not to worry about me, I could just roam around, and I will certainly find them. Then Mary told Joseph the lady had a place for us, it was a barn where she kept her animals, but it would provide a roof over their heads, and mine! A barn, that's perfect, we can all stay together. We walked down to the barn, and Joseph opened the door, and there were animals in there. They all looked at Mary then they looked at me then back to Mary. They all retreated back as to make a place for Mary. They were bowing. They claimed they were in the presence of greatness. I was a little troubled because they didn't know any of us, so how could they know? The little child was very special. I felt they were a little envious of my assignment. I was escorting this very special family and their great child. I was indeed humbled and grateful. This was my mission in life, to be of service to this wonderful family! And for them, I would give my very life.

We got settled in. Joseph made the best of what he had. He immediately made a place for Mary to lay down and rest. Then, he started to gather wood around the barn, and I could see he was about to create something wonderful. And he did, he made a little crib for the baby to lay on. It was a little manger with hay, but it was perfect. Joseph stepped out for a minute when suddenly we heard a baby's cry. Instantly the whole barn was filled with light, but a light so bright, it was nothing anyone had ever seen. Coming in and out of the light were beings; angels were abound. This was indeed a spectacular sight! Angel voices singing in adoration surrounding Mary and the baby. Can't even formulate words to describe what was happening. Joseph came in and saw what we were seeing. He fell to his knees. He praised God, and he was filled with joy. He approached Mary and the baby, and the angels just embraced them all. The power of God, our Creator, was indeed in this place.

Mary didn't rest much because shortly after there were knocks on the door, and shepherds came to see the baby. They told them about the choir of angels that announced the baby's birth to them and they just had to come. They told us about the bright star in the heavens and how it is now above this place. We went outside to see and low and behold the most of magnificent stars was hovering right above us. More shepherds kept coming and then just common people who had heard about the things that were happening. They brought gifts, the best of what they had. They brought sheep, they brought grain and fruits and bread and some even brought blankets and clothing for the baby. We lacked nothing. Joseph and Mary were overjoyed. The owner of the barn let us stay put for as long as we needed. She didn't even charge anything, but Mary and Joseph shared their abundance of gifts with her.

Joseph found a little place for us to live, and I felt we were going to stay put for a while. This was good. People had started to return home to their own towns, and Bethlehem started to feel like our new home. The star that had been seen above the barn had moved and was now directly above our new place. Everyone marveled at the sight and could not quite understand its significance. Joseph and Mary did though.

One day, I was looming about when I see a multitude of people coming towards me. I couldn't quite understand what was happening. These were caravans of some very important people and there were a lot of people. I thought they must be going the wrong way. King Herod's palace is in the other direction. I saw them pointing at the bright star and they kept coming. They stopped right in front of our house and knocked with such authority I thought the door was going to fall off. Joseph opened the door and let the leaders in, they looked like kings. I made my way closer to the door and saw the kings bowing down before the baby. They, too, brought gifts, many gifts, and Joseph and Mary were very humbled by the presence of these men.

After the visit, they set up camp nearby, and we thought that they would come back to visit the baby again. But, in the middle of the night, I was awakened by strange noises, and when I went exploring, I saw that all the caravans that had visited us were getting ready to leave. This was very strange because they didn't seem to be in any hurry before. The next day that was all everyone was talking about, and they wondered what might have caused them to leave so abruptly. Soon enough, I had a good idea, because shortly thereafter, I was awakened in the middle of the night by Joseph. We had another assignment! I'm ready to go wherever, but I was liking Bethlehem and my new friends. Joseph said, we would be going on a very long journey this time. We had to go to Egypt. I have never heard of the place but trusted there was a good reason we were going there. In no time at all, we left, leaving behind many of the gifts that had been offered to us. Everything was left behind for the owners of the barn and our house. That was their recompense for their generosity. We left Bethlehem by ourselves and walked most of the night until we joined up with a small caravan going to Egypt. Everyone kept saying how far it was and that it would take us months to get there, but there were guides along the way. The journey was difficult, but I had the pleasure of carrying Mary and the baby Jesus most of the way. We walked, and rested, and walked some more. A few times, I didn't know if I would make it, but I did.

Egypt is an incredible place. Sometimes we would see these enormous buildings which were things to marvel at, yet I sensed that these buildings were troublesome to Joseph and Mary. And, as Jesus grew up, He, too, had some sadness whenever He saw those buildings. I later learned of the difficult lives of their ancestors when they were slaves in this country many centuries ago.

Jesus and I had a beautiful relationship. He was my friend, and I was His. We played together, and I was always following Him wherever He went. He spent a lot of time praying and going to the temple. His favorite time was to just find a quite spot and pray. I think angels visited Him often because you could just feel the presence of God with Him all the time. We settled in well in Egypt and lived peaceful with everyone around us. Joseph, Mary, and Jesus kept their traditions alive and always followed their religious celebrations. God was first and foremost always.

This is the longest place we had lived in so far. This was the place I thought I was going to die. But God had yet another assignment for me. Joseph said that we were to return back to Judea. I could sense Joseph felt bad telling me we had to make that long journey back. I hopped and trotted about as to assure Him I was good. I am happy just to be where they are. Joseph smiled, and Jesus was excited. He wanted so much to go to Judea. There was where He was supposed to be. I was happy to take Him there!

The trip back was much better than that first time. The roads were better, the caravan was much better organized, and there were places along the way to rest more comfortably. Jesus was just enjoying the journey. He couldn't wait to get to Judea to see all the places His parents had told him about.

When we got to Judea, I thought we were going back to Bethlehem, but as we got closer, Joseph said, "We were going to Nazareth." That was definitely home. We returned to our old home. Mary's mother had already passed, and it was a little sad. We settled in well back in our home. Jesus helped out Joseph in His shop, and He and I would go looking for wood into the fields. I knew this land very well. Jesus was growing so strong and full of life.

Every year, we traveled to Jerusalem to celebrate the feast of the Passover, but after a few days, we would always return home. One day, however, when Jesus was about 12, we were getting ready to leave Jerusalem, and Mary had asked some friends if they had seen Jesus. She was told He was ahead of us with His friends. I had lost sight of Him when He went into the temple because Joseph had pulled me over to the side to load me up for our trip. Jesus was a little man now, and He wasn't riding me anymore; He preferred to walk alongside me now. I was waiting for Him to come and lead me on. But, when our friends had said He was ahead of us, there was no cause for concern. I walked along for several hours, and at the first rest stop, Mary wanted to keep going to go check on Jesus. Joseph kept walking faster, and when he returned, he said that he saw some of Jesus' friends who told him He was with other friends well ahead of us. The caravan picked up again, and hours later, when we should take a rest, Mary, Joseph, and I just kept walking asking for Jesus. We kept being told He was ahead of us. We kept walking and finally had to set up camp for the night. Mary didn't sleep all night. She kept going from place to place. In the morning, we were again assured someone had just seen Him ahead of us. We walked in haste. Mary and Joseph couldn't think of anything else but finding Jesus. They started thinking something had happened to Him. Was He sick, was He hurt, had He fallen? Jesus was not one to just disappear. Mary's face said it all. She was not resting until she found Jesus, until she had Him right in front of her. I did my part. I searched everywhere I could. I heard someone tell Joseph that they hadn't seen Jesus since Jerusalem. They were pretty sure He was not ahead of us. Finally, Mary couldn't go any further. She wanted to return to Jerusalem. She told Jesus' friends, families, and her own family members that if they saw Jesus to just keep him in their sight. She was returning to Jerusalem. She had to find him. Now, more and more people kept telling her that actually, the last time they saw him, He was either going to or He was in the temple. Mary knew the temple was truly Jesus' home, and so she wanted to go find Him. We had already been traveling for a day and a half, and it was going to take us just as long to return to Jerusalem. And, we did, directly to the temple. I stayed outside, but I could not believe my eyes when I saw the overwhelming joy of Mary and Joseph embracing Jesus as they came out of the temple. That day, I knew things had changed for this family.

Back in Nazareth, Jesus grew up to be a strong healthy young man. After Joseph passed, Jesus became the man of the house. He cared for his mother with so much love and affection, and the two spent hours praying and going over scripture. Everything came alive for them. Jesus took over Joseph's carpentry business and supported us. He was even a more skillful carpenter than Joseph. He had had a great teacher! Joseph and Mary had told Jesus all that had happened to them and how things came to be and what had been foretold about Him – His mission in life. And Jesus lived, prayed, and loved preparing for the day when God, His Father, would call Him to commence to fulfill His mission in life.

What better life has any animal lived than mine? My mission in life was to help, however slight, the Creator of the universe fulfill His plan on Earth!

What is this telling me?
How does it apply to my life?
What have I learned about Jesus here?

6.

WHERE DO WE GO FROM HERE?

As I inserted my inspirational moments here, I felt the Donkey was
a good ending. It tied up the early days of Jesus. When I was led to
advance to the next chapter in the Bible, I received messages as John
the Baptist, Jesus after His Baptism, and Jesus being led to the desert
and tempted by Satan. Just as I wrote those messages, Lenten 2020
season was fast approaching. I felt I needed to continue reading the
gospels but skip right to the passion of Christ, get into the spirit of
the season. I jumped right into all four gospels, identifying the
readings relating to the passion of Jesus. This became my Lenten
prayer. Again, I read and re-read different chapters. The first character to come through was Jesus' Guardian Angel when Jesus was
praying at the Garden of Gethsemane. Then, Judas came, the Servant who had his ear cut off came, Peter also made his way, as did
Joseph of Arimethea. I wrote them all down. Then, no characters
came through. I kept reading, praying, waiting, and hoping for Pilate, a soldier – there were so many characters who could come
through, but nothing. Then, while in prayer, I was reminded to look
back in my old journals, from 2012 and 2013, and see what I had
written down at the time when I meditated on the Stations of the

Cross. I did, and I was surprisingly amazed at the inspirations then. I have shared some of those inspirational messages with only a few people. The response has been the same to the messages here, although I do not feel that I am to share those in this book. Perhaps I can be a pencil in God's Hand, reflecting on His Suffering and Passion.

The Lenten season has come and gone. On Good Friday, our family experienced a tremendous loss with the passing of my brother-in-law Lourenço, but we were strengthen with the realization that he died in good company. What a blessed time, to be joined with Jesus in His death, confident that he would rise with Him on His Glorious Day! Lourenço died, knowing he was well loved by his whole family and well respected by all who knew him. His life was truly a gift to ours. As is customary in our faith, after someone dies, we pray the Rosary together for nine days. Even in the confines of the Coronavirus pandemic, we found ways to pray the Rosary together. Most inspiring was that the young grandchildren were always eager to pray the Rosary for Lourenco's soul and for our world today. Furthermore, for those who know and pray the Rosary, you can see how five of the inspirational messages here are meditations on the joyful mysteries.

As I share these inspirational moments, I do not want to be presumptions that I am somehow special. I am a sinner, learning to be open to God's guidance in my life. I truly feel that God wants me to share these inspirational moments, and so I obey.